W9-BCP-183

BRAVE GIRLS
Beautiful You

Written by
JENNIFER GERELDS

A Division of Thomas Nelson Publishers

Other Books in the Brave Girls Brand

Brave Girls Holy Bible

Brave Girls Bible Stories

Brave Girls: Better Than Perfect

Brave Girls: Faithful Friends

Contents

He has made everything beautiful in its time.

Ecclesiastes 3:11 NKJV

What *is* beautiful?

When Gracie, Hope, and I (Glory) asked each other that question, we were surprised by how different our answers were. The idea of *beautiful* made me think of deep, lovely colors with sparkle and shine, like the perfect party dress or twinkling stars in a dark night sky.

But my (Hope) first thought was of a brand-new, leather baseball glove, since I love sports so much. Then I thought maybe *beautiful* is more like when my brothers and I are getting along and having fun together.

And I (Gracie) had a totally different picture. I immediately thought of the models I've seen on magazine covers and some of my favorite movie stars. I mean, isn't that what everyone thinks beautiful is? At least that's what I thought at first . . .

So it was pretty clear to us that the idea of beauty can mean different things to different people. Who's right?

We didn't know, but we figured that God—the Creator of everything beautiful—could probably help us get to the bottom of what true beauty is. So we started praying for wisdom and looking all throughout the Bible to see what He says.

His answer amazed us! In this spectacular world filled with color, creativity, and originality, do you know what God sees as most beautiful of all?

His kids!

God thinks we are completely awesome because the Spirit of His beautiful Son, Jesus, lives inside each person who trusts in Him. No matter how quirky you may think your body or personality is, having the Spirit of God living inside you transforms your life into something out-of-this-world gorgeous. It's the ultimate makeover!

When you put your trust in Jesus, His love shines out of you and lights up the world—like a candle in a dark room. And that love frees you to be *exactly* the person God designed you to be, without

having to look a certain way or be like everybody else. You're beautiful because God created you and is making you more like His Son, Jesus, every day!

Want to know how? Then spend the next ninety days with us and discover how God made you in the most perfect way possible, to show off just how wonderful He is—in *beautiful you!*

—Glory, Hope, and Gracie

Glory Gracie Hope

BEAUTY BASICS

I f you know me, then you know how much I just *loooooove* girly things like pageants, dress-up parties, perfect outfits, and a really good updo (that's a fancy hairstyle, for those of you not into that kind of thing!). I love beautiful things because they make my heart happy in a way that's hard to explain. When I see something beautiful, it's like I want to become a part of it. Since everything beautiful comes from God, I guess it's His way of helping me see Him, appreciate Him, and want to know more about Him.

In this next section, I hope you'll learn to see—maybe for the first time—all the beautiful gifts you have in your life if you belong to Jesus. Our connection with Him not only takes away our sin but also adds all kinds of beautiful things to our lives—like being

 adopted into God's family forever and being promised a home in heaven for all of eternity. Belonging to God brings amazing color, beauty, and joy into our everyday lives. Simply opening our eyes to see the beauty God has placed all around us helps Him transform us into the beautiful people He has created us to be.

—Glory

Yes, I am sure that nothing can separate
us from the love God has for us.

Romans 8:38

How do you *know* when you are loved? Write some of the times you have felt loved: _when I get hurt and mymom puts on a bandag and kisses it_

When do you feel loved? Is it when you get hurt and your mom or dad puts a bandage on you and holds you close? Is it when your best friend stops what she's doing to listen to you? Is it being forgiven when you've messed up?

Love can show itself in a million different ways, but it always has the same effect: it makes us feel warm, safe, important, and secure. But because people are sinners, they can't always love perfectly. It might even seem like some people might stop loving you altogether if you aren't good enough.

But God isn't like that. The Bible says God *is* love. And because you are God's child, He gives you the greatest and most forever kind of love you could possibly have—He loves you like He loves Jesus. Best of all, nothing—not even death—can separate us from God's love. No matter what happens, His kids are always safe, important, and secure. God's love never ends. There's nothing more beautiful than that.

Prayer Pointer

God, help me believe that Your love for me
never changes and that it lasts forever.

Beauty Reborn

IF ANYONE belongs to CHRIST, THEN HE is made NEW.
THE old THINGS HAVE gONE; eveRyTHiNG is made NEW!

2 CoRiNTHiaNs 5:17

What would you like for your birthday? Circle the items that interest you:

- new clothes
- old tennis shoes
- a new art set
- used pencils
- a new phone
- your brother's old basketball

You probably didn't pick any of the old stuff. Birthdays are supposed to celebrate life and new beginnings. People give new and special gifts for birthdays, not old or worn-out things.

God feels the same way about birthdays. When you were born, you were new and beautiful and full of life. However, you were also born under the curse of sin that started when Adam and Eve disobeyed God. As you grow older, and God opens your heart to believe that Jesus is the Savior and your only hope for heaven, something amazing happens. Your spirit is born again! It's like a new birthday, and God has gifts for you.

You might not look new on the outside, but inside, God makes you an entirely new creation by sending His Spirit to live inside you. The Spirit empowers you to pray, read the Bible, and understand God better. Best of all, it guarantees your place in heaven with Jesus forever!

PRayeR PoiNteR

Father, thank You for making me a
beautiful, new creation in Jesus!

Planned with Purpose

I pRaise you because you made me in
an amazing and wonderful way.

Psalm 139:14

Have you ever just sat and watched people at the mall or at a football game? What are some things you've noticed that make people different from each other?

Isn't God's creativity amazing? While everybody might look kind of the same in magazines, in real life people come in different shapes, sizes, and personalities. Noticing all those differences can be fun. But sometimes watching other people can have a bad effect on you. That's because it's tempting to look at others and think they're smarter, funnier, prettier, or more talented. We can even start to think they're better than we are and that we'll never be as special as they are.

But that's not true! God says in Psalm 139 that He carefully crafted each of us just exactly as He had planned before He even created the world. That means you are specially designed by God to display His genius and brilliant creativity in a way *only you* can! We were each made to be uniquely beautiful stars in this wonderful universe He has made.

And since God's creative and powerful Spirit lives in you, who knows what wild and wonderful purpose God has planned for your life? With God as your guide and power, not even the sky is the limit!

PRayeR PoiNteR

Jesus, thank You for making me perfectly
unique to show Your glory.

5

No one can build any other foundation.
The foundation that has already
been laid is Jesus Christ.

1 Corinthians 3:11

Look at the list of clothes and jewelry below and number them in the order you would put them on:

☐ necklace   ☐ bracelet

☐ scarf   ☐ boots

☒ your favorite shirt and jeans

Did you put a number one by your favorite shirt and jeans? You should! Because all those other things are the accessories that go on top. A great outfit starts with a great foundation—like your favorite shirt and jeans. Then you can add all the extra accessories—like scarves, jewelry, and boots—to make a beautiful, stylish outfit. Believe it or not, the same principle applies to our spiritual lives. Good behaviors like nice manners, working hard, and being kind to others are like a wardrobe of beautiful accessories. But for true spiritual beauty, you need more than accessories; you need a great foundation.

So what's step one in God's beauty process? Jesus. He is our foundation—not just for what we wear, but for our whole lives. His Spirit inside us is what changes our hearts to help us obey His Word and become beautiful. Once we belong to God and the Holy Spirit lives in us, then we can apply the truths that God says will make us

beautiful in His sight—things like loving and giving, sharing and forgiving.

For instance, instead of staying mad at your friend who didn't invite you over for her slumber party, you can forgive and love her. Instead of demanding your parents give you whatever you want, you can look for ways to spend your time, money, or talents to help people in need. With Jesus' love encouraging us and making us strong, we can follow His example. That kind of beauty is always in style!

Prayer Pointer

Jesus, I need You to fill me and strengthen me
completely so that I can be beautiful like You.

Our physical body is becoming older
and weaker, but our spirit inside
us is made new every day.

2 Corinthians 4:16

Have you ever been in the makeup aisle at the store? Hundreds of products line the shelves, promising to make girls more beautiful. There is every kind of powder, cream, and lotion imaginable, and they all promise to make you look beautiful. But real beauty doesn't come in a jar or a tube. Real beauty is becoming who God wants you to be—and it happens from the inside out.

God is slowly changing us on the inside . . . from the ugliness of our sin to the beautiful goodness of His Son, Jesus. The more we trust and obey God, the more we realize how much we need Jesus and the more beautiful our character becomes. We actually begin to think, talk, and act more like Jesus and less like our old, selfish selves. Our love for God and our love for others grow. As it grows, a miracle happens: we become beautiful mirrors of God's never-ending affection for His people.

True beauty can't be bought in the makeup aisle. True beauty only comes from loving Jesus. This kind of beauty not only shines in our dark world but also lasts for all eternity in heaven with Jesus.

Prayer Pointer

Lord, change me from the inside out. Please
make me Your kind of beautiful forever.

Safe and Secure

God Has said, "I will NeveR leave
you; I will NeveR abaNdoN you."

HebRews 13:5

Have you ever gotten lost in a store or separated from your parents? One minute you were exploring all the new clothes, feeling safe and fine. The next minute, you looked up and found yourself all alone—and all those good feelings vanished. Panic set in as you wandered up and down aisles, hoping to find your mom and dad so you could feel safe again.

Sometimes we feel that way even when we aren't lost. When we have to face hard times—like a family member getting sick or dying, parents getting divorced, or friends moving away—we can get that same lost and lonely feeling. Jesus' followers felt the same way when He was crucified, and they felt that way again when He rose up into heaven.

But Jesus didn't want them to feel alone, and He doesn't want us to either. He promised that He will never leave us—and He doesn't! When we accept Jesus as our Savior, He puts His Spirit inside us. So no matter where we go or what we do, Jesus is right there with us. We are never lost to God. Feelings of loneliness and sadness are just signals for us to stop and remember that He is still with us—even if we can't see Him—and that we are safe in His never-ending love for us.

PRayeR PoiNteR

Jesus, thank You for always being
with me—now and forever.

God loves the person who gives happily. And God can give you more blessings than you need.

2 Corinthians 9:7-8

Picture this: You have been saving your money for weeks to buy those supercute boots you've been wanting forever. Then one Sunday, a lady comes to your church and tells everybody that the children's home in your city is having trouble. They don't have enough money to support all the orphans. What do you think God would want you to do?

A. Ignore the request.
B. Pray that someone else with more money pitches in.
C. Give some of your money while keeping some for yourself.
D. Hand it all over to the lady.

It's not an easy question to answer, is it? God tells us that taking care of the poor, orphans, and widows is very important to Him. He also says that He loves cheerful givers because giving to others shows them His kind of love in a very real way that they can understand. When we ask God what He'd like us to do and then we obey Him, our faith and love grow stronger. It's wonderful knowing that we are joining God in His important work of showing people that He loves them. And we know that He will always take care of our needs too (even if it means having to wait a little while longer for those supercute boots!).

Prayer Pointer

Lord, please help me trust You to take care of me so that I can cheerfully give to others.

Home Sweet Home

Before the world was made, God decided to make us His own children through Jesus Christ.

Ephesians 1:5

Imagine visiting a friend at her family's beautiful home. It's filled with comfy furniture and the smell of freshly baked cookies. Then your friend welcomes you into the kitchen and asks if you'd like something to eat. Everything is so wonderful. You wish that it all belonged to you—that you could stay forever.

Now imagine the same scene, but this time the house really *is* yours. *You* open the fridge and find something wonderful to give to your guests. You don't just feel at home; you *are* home. So what's the difference?

Everything! Being someone's guest can be fun, but at some point you know you'll have to leave and go back to your own house. But when you're a part of the family who owns the beautiful home, you can stay there forever. You never have to leave, and you are always welcome.

That's what it's like when you accept Jesus as your Savior. God, your heavenly Father, adopts you, and you become part of the greatest royal family in the universe. Your place in God's kingdom is permanent because God never leaves His kids. All the benefits and blessings of His kingdom are yours for the taking . . . and for offering to your guests who just might become future family members too.

Prayer Pointer

Thank You, Jesus, for welcoming me into
Your beautiful family forever!

> But Lord, you are our father.
> We are like clay, and you are the
> potter. Your hands made us all.
>
> Isaiah 64:8

Have you ever worked with clay on a potter's wheel? First, you place your lump of clay onto the center of the wheel. Then you gently press into the center with your thumbs as the wheel turns, using your other fingers to shape the outside, forming a bowl, a cup, or a vase.

Gradually, you can form a bowl or a vase that can be dried or fired in a kiln to make it stronger. It is a slow and steady process, but a beautiful piece of art can be created from a lump of clay. That's pretty amazing!

Creating is fun, isn't it? God thinks so too. He says that people are like clay, and He is the Potter. Just like He formed Adam from the dust of the ground, He shapes who we are. He presses in—using our family, school, teachers, church, and all kinds of experiences, even the bad ones—to mold us and make us fit for the purpose He has planned for us. We might not always like the molding and shaping part, and we might even wonder sometimes if God knows what He's doing . . . but He always does!

Your life is safe in God's hands. Instead of fighting the way He is shaping you, open your eyes and heart to His plans for you—they'll always be perfectly designed. Then, thank Him for making you ready for the beautiful purpose He has for your life.

Prayer Pointer

Father, I trust You to use every moment in my life to shape me into the person You want me to be.

You are living with crooked and mean
people all around you. Among them you
shine like stars in the dark world. You offer
to them the teaching that gives life.

Philippians 2:15–16

It's time for a trip out into the country where the man-made streetlights end and the beautiful lights of the night sky begin. If you find the right spot, you'll be able to see the heavens stretching overhead like a dark, velvet blanket dotted with brilliant sparkles of light. Individually, each star is only a tiny light in the great big darkness of the night sky. Together, the lights join to brighten up the whole night sky, shining all the way down to earth.

God says that believers are just like those shining stars. Lit up by God's Spirit inside us, our lives look very different from the dark world all around us. The Bible calls people who do not believe in God "lost"; they cannot find a lasting purpose or meaning in life. List below some of the things of this world that people look to for happiness instead of looking to God:

Some people look at their own happiness instead of God.

When people look to the things of the world for happiness, they will always be disappointed—never finding joy, peace, or true life. Their world will be dark. But those people who belong to God have the light of Jesus' hope. We have been forgiven, saved, and honored by God. And we have love to give because we have been loved first. As we show others what it means to know Jesus, His light shines out of us, pierces the darkness of this world, and draws other people to Him.

Prayer Pointer

Father, thank You for filling me with Your light so
I can show lasting joy to others around me.

Free to Fail

Those who are in Christ Jesus are not judged guilty.

Romans 8:1

"It's not my fault!" Alyssa yelled defensively, looking at the burned cookies her mother just pulled out of the oven.

"Well, if you hadn't turned the TV up so loud, you would've heard the buzzer," replied her mother.

"You guys always blame me for everything!" Alyssa cried, stomping off to her room.

The truth is, Alyssa was given a task, and she failed to do it correctly. Has that ever happened to you? How did you react?

None of us like to admit when we've done something wrong. We may be afraid that we will be judged, we will get in trouble, or people will stop liking us. We may also worry that God will give up on us too, especially if we keep making the same mistake or repeating the same sin over and over again.

But God already knows your whole story, and He loves you anyway. Why? Because His Son, Jesus, has already paid the price for all the sins you've ever committed or ever will commit. You aren't guilty anymore. You are a forgiven child of God who can bravely come to the Father with all your mistakes and mess-ups because He *always* accepts you—in Jesus. The beauty of mistakes is that they can actually help us realize how much we really need Jesus for everything.

Prayer Pointer

Thank You, Jesus, for covering all my sins
and making me right with God forever.

Lovely Light

> "All people will know that you are my
> followers if you love each other."
>
> JOHN 13:35

If someone asked you to describe a Christian, what would you say? Chances are you'd mention things like "reads the Bible and prays," "goes to church," or even "does lots of good things for people." Those are all signs that people might have given their lives to Jesus. But when you think about it, lots of people who don't claim to be Christians live good lives. Many other religions teach that you have to do good works and stay away from bad behaviors . . . so they also spend a *lot* of time doing good things and staying out of trouble.

But Jesus says that His children must be identified by something more. He says people will know us because of our love—love for Jesus, love for other believers, and love for those who don't know Him. The ability to love like that comes from the Holy Spirit, who lives inside us.

Ask God to help you consider your words before you say them and your actions before you do them, and make sure they show His love. God will pour out His love *to* you and *through* you to reach others who need to know Him. And everyone will know you're one of His children by your lovely light of love.

PRayeR PointeR

Jesus, fill me with Your love for others
so they will see You in me.

Beautiful Fragrance

THe smell of youR peRfume is pleasaNt. YouR
Name is pleasaNt like expeNsive peRfume!

Song of Songs 1:3

What do you love to smell? Circle your favorites below:

- cookies baking in the oven
- your dad's cologne
- cut grass
- French fries
- Christmas trees
- your mom's perfume
- new crayons

As you thought about each of these scents, did they remind you of special memories? Our sense of smell is so strong that it often creates our strongest and most lasting memories. Certain fragrances become permanently linked in our minds to particular places, times, and people in our lives.

God says that our love for Him is like a powerful perfume that He remembers *forever*. So how can we show God we love Him? In all kinds of colorful, creative, and beautiful ways, just like a bouquet of flowers. Spending time with Him in prayer, singing songs, studying His Word, and thinking about and thanking Him for His goodness—these are all wonderful ways to show God your love.

Then, as your relationship with Him grows stronger, something amazing happens. The people around you begin to notice the fragrance of Christ! They notice when you choose to help with a service project at church instead of going to see a movie with your friends, or when you help with a fund-raiser for people hurt by a natural disaster. They see a difference in you when you go out of

your way to say something encouraging to a kid who is sad, or when you help the cafeteria ladies clean up a mess you didn't make. They begin to link your kindness and love toward others with the God you are telling them about.

Before you know it, they'll be giving their lives to God, and He'll use them to spread the fragrance of His love too!

PRAYER POINTER

Lord, please make my life a beautifully fragrant perfume in Your world.

> You are being built into a place where
> God lives through the Spirit.
>
> Ephesians 2:22

Picture in your mind a big, beautiful house. Everything looks lovely, but when you look closer, you realize the walls are cracked and they aren't securely connected to the floor—or to each other! How long could a wobbly house like that stand?

You don't have to be a construction expert to know that a safe, strong house has to have a good foundation with walls and a roof that connect and hold everything together. Because if they don't, the whole thing will fall in on itself!

Jesus tells us that He is the builder of His kingdom and that each one of His people is like a brick in the great kingdom He's building. He is the cornerstone and foundation that everything is built on, and His Spirit is the mortar sticking us all together. Each of us is important in this grand work that God is doing.

We weren't made to stand alone or apart from God or other Christians. If we keep to ourselves, we create a hole where our presence is really needed. We can best understand our purpose when we stay in friendship with God and His people. Working together, we can do God's will and grow into a safe, strong fortress where others can clearly see God's love and glory.

Prayer Pointer

Thank You, God, for making me a part of Your big plan
and connecting me with Your people for Your glory.

Crown of Creation

God looked at everything He had made, and it was very good.

Genesis 1:31

Can you imagine what it was like in those first days of creation? With just a word, God filled the once-empty space with the most beautiful trees and plants, grass and mountains. Then He made the animals—the sweet, fuzzy kind and the great big, towering giant kind. Through the power of His incredible creativity, God made a spectacular world filled with life and color and beauty. Each day, after He made something, He looked at it and said that it was good.

But that's not what He said after He made Adam and Eve, His first two people, on the sixth day of creation. This time He said, "It's *very* good!"

From the beginning of time, God has been in love with His people. We are the crown on top of all the beauty He has made. Even when sin entered the world, God's view of us didn't change. He wanted us to stay close to Him, so much that He sent His own precious Son to die for our sins, making it possible for us to be God's kids forever! That means that nothing can change God's mind about how great you are to Him. Each one of God's children is His special treasure, a reflection of His glory, and the receiver of His never-ending love.

Prayer Pointer

Thank You, Jesus, for giving me such a special
and honored place in Your heart.

RADIANT REFLECTIONS

I used to hate looking in the mirror. I felt like my hair was the wrong color, my nose was too small, and my legs looked like they belonged on a chicken. But then something really incredible started happening in my mind after I got involved with our church's youth group. I listened to the stories the leaders told us about Jesus. Then I began to read them for myself, and I was amazed. Jesus loved *everyone*, not just the people who seemed perfect. He saw beauty in the people society saw as only sinners. He saw the sick as people worth healing. He saw the offerings of the poor as something beautiful and generous. He saw people without wisdom or understanding, and He wanted to be their shepherd.

Our youth leaders also talked about how when we look in a mirror, we see who we are. But when we look at the life of Jesus and the truth He taught, we see who God is making us to be.

Suddenly, I realized I'd been looking at myself all wrong when I didn't like what I saw in the mirror. I was focusing on all the things I thought were wrong with me. But when I look at myself as Jesus does, I see myself—and the world around me—in a whole new light. I see beauty in myself and in others where I have never seen it before, and it makes me want to celebrate and to help others see their beauty too. So this section is to help you see yourself as beautiful—just like our Savior, Jesus, does.

—Gracie

Like Father, Like Son

No one has seen God, but Jesus
is exactly like Him.

Colossians 1:15

The disciples had walked and worked and lived with Jesus for three years. They had seen His miracles firsthand: fish and bread multiplied to feed thousands, the sick healed, the lame walking, the blind seeing, the dead coming back to life. They had heard Jesus' teaching, and they had learned about God. Peter himself had already declared that Jesus was the Christ, the Son of the living God.

But when Jesus began to talk about His upcoming death on the cross, the disciples were confused and scared. They must have thought, *What will we do without our leader? What will happen to us and to the ministry?* So Philip piped up. He said, "Lord, show us the Father. That is all we need." In other words, "Jesus, stop messing around and let us see God now. Then this won't be so scary."

Jesus' answer shocked them: "He who has seen me has seen the Father" (John 14:8–9).

Have *you* ever wondered what God looks like? Jesus let Philip—and you—know that God the Father looks just like Jesus because they are One in spirit. Seeing Jesus' life and love is like seeing God's reflection. When we know and love what we see in Jesus, we are knowing and loving God the Father too.

Prayer Pointer

Father, thank You for showing Yourself to us
through Jesus' life on earth.

THe LoRd is tHe God wHo lives foRevR.
He cReated all tHe woRld. . . . No oNe caN
undeRstand How gReat His wisdom is.

Isaiah 40:28

In the space provided below, draw something spectacular.

Was it hard to come up with ideas? Now imagine for a moment what it must have been like for God before He ever created the earth. Talk about a blank canvas! It was total emptiness. Then God spoke what was in His mind, and the most amazing creation appeared. He placed all the stars and planets in just the right spots, to spin and travel in orbits, with the perfect balance of gravity keeping everything in order. Then He zeroed in on earth, crafting every tiny blade of grass, every great creature, and every breathtaking landscape

that exists. Take a few minutes to step outside and look at how different each plant is, how vast the sky is, how amazing the wind is as it whistles through trees. It's overwhelming! God is beyond genius, and His creativity goes beyond our ability to understand.

That same creative God *lives in you*. When you risk sharing your true thoughts in a poem or song, you are reflecting His creativity. When you draw or paint with all your best effort, you mirror God's flair for beauty and color. And when you boldly share something God has taught you through His Word, you are helping the world see His glory in a brilliant, new way.

Prayer Pointer

God, please help me share Your love
with the world in creative ways.

"Do You Love Me?"

Counsel in the heart of man is like deep water,
But a man of understanding will draw it out.

PROVERBS 20:5 NKJV

Peter had blown it in the worst way imaginable. After spending years with Jesus, he abandoned his Lord when the soldiers came to arrest Jesus. Peter had promised to stay by Jesus' side, but instead he ran away in fear and told everyone who asked that he didn't even know Him.

After Jesus was crucified and rose again, He appeared to Peter. Now, if you were the one who had been deserted and betrayed instead of Jesus, what would you have said to Peter?

Jesus didn't say, "I told you so" or "You're a terrible friend." Instead, He asked Peter a question: "Do you love me?"

His question reached deep into Peter's heart. Peter thought about it and said, "Yes, I love you."

"Then feed my sheep," answered Jesus. Jesus was telling Peter that he was forgiven, and if he loved Him, then he needed to take care of the people who loved Jesus.

Jesus asks you the same question. "Do you love Me, Brave Girl?" To answer truthfully, like Peter, you have to think about it and be completely honest. If the answer is yes, then you too are completely forgiven. Now Jesus wants you to join Him in His work of bringing lost sheep to the Great Shepherd.

Prayer Pointer

I want to truly love You, Lord. Please help me
show it by obeying and following You.

Trading Treasures

"Don't store treasures for yourselves here on earth. . . . Store your treasure in heaven."
Matthew 6:19-20

People spend years going to school to become doctors. It takes a lot of money, hard work, and time to get a degree that allows you to take care of others. So it would make sense for doctors to work where they will make the most money, right?

But some doctors don't. Instead, they look for places in poor countries where the people get no medical help. They go to those places, even though they might never get a penny for what they do! Why would anyone do that? To live like Jesus.

Jesus left the comfort and glory of heaven to come to earth and save His people. His heart was filled with compassion for all the people who were hurting and needed healing, both physically and spiritually. Jesus made Himself poor so that people could be made rich in God.

Whenever we help other people who are hurting, we are showing Jesus' love to the world. If you choose to sit beside someone who is lonely to cheer her up, if you visit the homeless and bring them food, if you raise money to help your local widows or orphans, you are living like Jesus did. Your actions and love tell the world that Jesus cares for them. And you are building up riches that last—in heaven.

Prayer Pointer

Jesus, help me care about people the same way You do.

> "You will know that I say only what
> the Father has taught me."

JOHN 8:28

Imagine that you are walking into a church gathering along with your parents, and it looks like you are the only kid in the group. Before you know it, some adults are walking up to your family, about to start a conversation. You have to decide quickly what you'll do. Circle below the best ways to respond:

A. Hide behind your parents.
B. Smile and say, "Hi! I'm _____."
C. Look down and don't answer any questions, hoping they will go away soon.
D. Turn to your parents and tell them you're ready to leave.
E. Stick out your hand for a handshake while looking them in the eye, saying, "I'm glad to meet you."

Chances are you know that B and E are the best answers because your parents or a teacher has taught you how to interact with others.

Jesus tells us that His Father, God, taught Him too. He prayed and talked to God all the time, and He listened to everything God told Him. He always knew what to do because He had learned everything from His Father. Jesus followed His Father's orders!

If we want to lead others to our heavenly Father just like Jesus

did, then we will need to spend time with God so we know who He is and what He wants. As we pray and study His Word, God's Spirit will give us the wisdom we need to talk and walk like Jesus.

Prayer Pointer

Lord, fill me with Your love and words so
I can show Your heart to others.

Be a woRkeR wHo is Not asHamed of
His woRk—a woRkeR wHo uses tHe tRue
teacHiNg iN tHe RigHt way.

2 TimotHy 2:15

W rite down all the reasons you love to do homework:

_____

_____

Are the spaces still empty? Don't worry. While some people love the challenge of reading difficult passages or discovering how the world operates, others would rather play a game or go out for a run. Yet all the adults around seem to think homework and studying are really important. Do you know why?

True, homework will help you get good grades—but that only scratches the surface. Guess who made the world you are studying about in school? God did! So when you study sea creatures or the amazing way plants produce food, you aren't just learning facts for a test. You're understanding a little bit more about the amazing God who made this world. You're getting glimpses into His power, perfection, sense of humor, and love. Add to that knowledge the truth about God in His Word, and you'll see how great God really is.

PRayeR PoiNteR

Jesus, help me study hard in school and in Your Word
so that I can learn more about You and Your world.

Early the next morning, Jesus woke and . . .
went to a place to be alone and pray.

Mark 1:35

When should you pray? Circle the scenarios that are most worthy of prayer:

- You are nervous about a test at school.
- You just won the spelling bee.
- You have just woken up in the morning.
- You are scared to share your faith.
- Your parent is sick.
- You yelled at your mom.

Did you circle them all? You should! God wants us to pray all the time—whether we're sad, scared, happy, unsure, excited, or mad. God created prayer as a way for us to have the closest relationship with Him possible. Through prayer, we invite God into every single part of our lives, sharing everything with Him and looking for Him to enjoy it with us or help us through it.

When we live prayer-filled lives, we are showing that we trust and love God the same way Jesus did when He was on earth. You might think that since Jesus *is* God He wouldn't need to pray. But Jesus prayed all the time and counted on His Father for everything. We need to depend on God the same way—through prayer.

Prayer Pointer

Jesus, thank You for inviting me to be
close to You through the gift of prayer.

> "I tell you that her many sins are forgiven. This is clear because she showed great love."

Luke 7:47

How much is too much to forgive? Circle the situations below that would be too hard to forgive:

- Your little brother broke your favorite game.
- Your best friend promised to keep your secret, but she didn't.
- Your parents got divorced.
- Your teacher embarrassed you in front of the class.

When someone wrongs us, we want to protect ourselves and punish that person by staying mad. We feel like it's our right to be mad because we are hurt. But God doesn't agree. One time, Peter asked Jesus how many times we are to forgive others. "Up to seven times?" he guessed. Jesus' answer surprised Peter. Jesus said, "Seven times seven." In other words, *every* time someone hurts us.

Why? Jesus explained it through a story about a merciful master who forgave a huge debt his servant owed him. But then that servant left and demanded another man pay him back the small debt that man owed. The master heard what his servant had done and was furious because the servant that he forgave didn't show mercy to others. In the same way, Jesus paid the huge debt we owe to God for our sin. Because He died in our place, we are totally

forgiven. Every time someone wrongs us, Jesus wants us to remember His goodness and mercy to us. If He forgives our great sin, how can we refuse to forgive others?

Prayer Pointer

Jesus, because You have forgiven me, I will also forgive others who wrong me.

> God, you will not reject a heart that
> is broken and sorry for its sin.

Psalm 51:17

The young woman knew she wasn't invited, but she came anyway. She entered the home of a well-known Pharisee—a religious leader who would hate her because of her bad reputation. She didn't care, though, because it wasn't his favor she wanted. She needed Jesus, who was the Pharisee's dinner guest.

When she came in the room, she broke open her jar of expensive perfume and poured it on Jesus' feet. Crying, she wiped her tears and the perfume from His feet with her hair. It was the perfect picture of a person who realized how unworthy she was and how thankful she was for Jesus' love and forgiveness. Jesus told her she was forgiven; her faith saved her.

Jesus says that God is not impressed by our success or popularity—or even how good other people think we are. He sees past all of that and looks inside our hearts. When we realize how sinful we are and how much we desperately need Jesus, God sees the beauty of our humble hearts and our dependence on Him. He then forgives our sins and welcomes us into a beautiful friendship with Him.

Prayer Pointer

Lord, You love it when I am honest about how much I
need You. It makes me love You and others more.

Serving One by One

*"I am making myself ready to serve.
I do this for them so that they can
truly be ready for your service."*

JOHN 17:19

I f someone wanted to be famous today, what do you think she'd do? Circle your answers below:

- run for a political office
- do something crazy to get noticed
- seek out the attention of large crowds
- spend most of her time with a few people

Which of those tactics did Jesus use? The last one on the list! It's not that Jesus didn't want the whole world to hear about Him, because He did. But Jesus didn't care about being famous. He wanted to bring real and lasting change to people's hearts. Instead of trying to get everyone to like Him, He chose to teach and train a handful of disciples. By living with them, walking with them, teaching them, and showing them the power of God, Jesus changed their lives. Those men then taught others . . . who taught others . . . who taught others. Like wildfire, the Word of God spread all over the world.

You don't have to be famous to make a difference in the world for Jesus. Just start praying and sharing God's love with the people around you. Then wait for God to do what only He can—change lives.

Prayer Pointer

Lord, help me see the beauty of spending time
with others and telling them about You.

I have fought the good fight. I have finished the race. I have kept the faith.

2 Timothy 4:7

On a scale of 1 to 10, rate yourself on how good you are at finishing a task you've been given.

1 2 3 4 5 6 7 8 9 10

Were you thinking, *Well, it depends on the task*? We are more than happy to keep playing that video game until we win. But studying for that test until we really understand the material? Or cleaning the top of the dresser *and* under the bed when cleaning our room? Persevering—that means sticking to a task until it's completely done—is easier when the reward is great.

Jesus understands. The task His Father had given Him wasn't easy at all: Leave heaven and all Your glory to go suffer on earth while You love and serve people. Then, finally, die a horrible and painful death.

Wow! That's a tough task! But Jesus felt the reward was worth it. He would rise again and return to His glory. He would save all the people who loved Him, and He would get to be with them forever in heaven. The task was hard, but it was worth it!

Life will not be easy for us either. But God calls us to persevere through every trial, looking to Him for help and trusting in His goodness. When we do, we show the patience and trust of Jesus at

work in our lives. Like our Savior, we will be rewarded with God's peace today and the promise of an eternity in heaven with Him and His people.

PRAyeR PoiNteR

Jesus, help me turn to You for strength
whenever I feel like giving up.

He Has taken ouR sins away fRom us
as faR as tHe east is fRom west.

Psalm 103:12

If you could go back in time and erase a mistake you've made that still bothers you to this day, what would it be? How would your life be different if you hadn't made that mistake or any mistakes at all? Sound too good to be possible?

The Samaritan woman who met Jesus at Jacob's well would have agreed. She had a lot of mistakes in her past, and almost everyone in town knew about them. But there wasn't anything she could do about them—until the day she met Jesus. Jesus told her she should ask Him for living water.

As she talked to Jesus, the Samaritan woman learned that He not only knew everything about her ruined past and even her current sins but also had the power to wash it all away. Excited that God had come and erased her guilty past, she ran to tell her whole village about the great news of Jesus and the living water she had found.

If you know Jesus, you don't have to carry around guilt over your mistakes. Jesus has washed your entire life clean and made you right with God forever. When you think about God's incredibly good news as the Samaritan woman did, you'll want to tell everyone you know too.

PRayeR PointeR

Jesus, thank You for freeing me from the guilt of
sin and making me beautiful in God's sight.

> You should take care of the needs of those who are troubled. Then your light will shine in the darkness.
>
> Isaiah 58:10

Have you ever had a cold? How about the flu? How did people react to being around you while you were sick? They probably didn't want to get too close because they were afraid they might get sick too. Back in Jesus' day, the Jews didn't want to be around sick or disabled people, for fear they might "catch" whatever those people had. For those who had long-lasting illnesses, like leprosy or the woman with unexplained bleeding, life was miserable. Not only were they sick, but people avoided them and treated them like they were cursed.

When Jesus began His ministry, He saw the poor and sick in a different light. Instead of avoiding them, He welcomed them. He touched and healed them. He never saw some people as better than others. He said they were all like lost sheep who needed Him, the Good Shepherd.

When you look at your family or the kids at school or people wherever you go, what do you see? Are you drawn more to the people who look good and are popular? Do you avoid those who don't fit in? Ask Jesus to help you see His beauty in everyone you meet. Then ask Him to make you brave enough to love both the greatest and the least with all your heart.

Prayer Pointer

Lord, help me see the beauty and value
in everyone You've made.

In youR lives you must tHiNk aNd
act like CHRist Jesus.

PHilippiaNs 2:5

Do you have a servant's heart? Circle the answer that best describes you.

1. When you come home from school and see dishes piled up in the sink, you:

  a. get a snack and then add your plate to the pile.
  b. run past the kitchen and hope your mom gets to them soon.
  c. take a few minutes to rinse the plates and load the dishwasher.

2. When a crowd of kids is loading into the van, you:

  a. call shotgun and try to ride up front.
  b. make sure you get a seat with your friends.
  c. offer to sit in the back so it's easier for everyone else to find a seat.

3. Saturdays are the perfect days for:

  a. sleeping late and watching TV.
  b. going to the mall and shopping.
  c. volunteering at the Children's Home.

Did you answer C for all of the above? If you did, your life is a beautiful example of how Jesus loved and served others. He set that

example for us when He, as God of the universe, humbled Himself to come to earth to help us.

One time, when Jesus was with His disciples, He showed how important humble service is to God. He took off His outer robes, picked up a servant's towel, and then washed His disciples' dirty, smelly feet. Peter was actually horrified that Jesus would stoop so low for him. But Jesus told Peter that all His people must humble themselves just like He had, and they must work hard to make life better and brighter for others. When we look for ways to serve others instead of ourselves, we shine God's light and love into a dark world, and we help people see the love of Jesus.

PRAYER POINTER

Jesus, help me humbly serve everyone You put into my life. Help me to have a servant's heart for You.

A Tempting Idea

WHEN you aRe tempted, God will also give you a way to escape tHat temptation.

1 CoRintHiaNs 10:13

Look at the list of temptations below and circle the ones you find hardest to fight:

- keeping the whole bag of candy for yourself instead of sharing
- telling that juicy bit of gossip you know about the new girl in school
- continuing to play your video game because you know your parents are distracted and won't know
- writing the answers to the test on your hand
- yelling at your siblings when they get on your nerves
- Write something else that tempts you here: _____

_____

_____

Sometimes it just feels *impossible* to make the right choice when everything inside us wants to cave in to temptation. After all, we're only human, right? Who could expect us to do the right thing in *that* situation?

Jesus could, that's who! But He isn't just standing around, waiting for you to mess up and judging you if you do. No, He says He understands exactly how you feel because when He was on earth,

He was tempted too. The only difference is that Jesus is God, and He was able to stand strong against every temptation. What that means for you is that Jesus knows not only how it feels to be tempted but also how to help you stand strong against temptations so that you can please God with your choices.

Whenever you turn to Jesus for help in the middle of a tempting situation, you are trusting in His secret source of strength: the goodness and power of God.

PRayeR PoiNteR

Jesus, thank You for understanding my weakness. Help me be strong in You.

WORKS OF BEAUTY

My family and I have served at one of our local soup kitchens for as long as I can remember. I really didn't think much about it. It was just what we did every first Saturday morning of the month, and each time we served food to mostly the same people.

But last Saturday something happened. One of the regulars took hold of my hand just before I was about to plop a spoonful of green beans on her plate. She looked me in the eyes and, in her raspy, quiet voice, she said, "Honey, you've got more than a scoop of green beans there. What you're doing gives me hope that God hasn't forgotten me yet."

I was shocked! I had never really thought that by simply serving other people, they could see and feel God's love. Suddenly serving green beans seemed like a spectacular privilege. By loving others well, we get to share the hope and joy that  always come from God. That's part of why He fills His kids with His beauty to begin with! This next section will help get your creative juices flowing to see all the different ways you can share the beauty of God's grace in the world around you too.

—Hope

Ripple Effect

"He who believes in me will do
the same things that I do."

JOHN 14:12

Have you ever thrown a rock into a still lake? If so, you've seen the "ripple effect." Rings of waves flow out from the spot where your rock landed, making bigger and bigger circles in the water until the waves reach the shore. It's amazing how one little rock can have such a big impact on a large body of water.

In a way, our world is a lot like that big lake. Our world seems too big and we seem too small for our lives to actually make an impact in it. But God doesn't see us that way. He uses everything we do, no matter how small, to reach places we never could've imagined.

What are some stones you can throw into your world for good? A few ideas are listed below; try adding some of your own. Then put them into action and see how God uses the ripple effect in your world.

Stone: Giving your mom an honest compliment and thanking her for her work.

Stone: Asking for donations to your favorite charity instead of Christmas gifts this year.

Stone: Praying every day for God to use you to spread His Word.

Stone: _____

Stone: _____

Prayer Pointer

Thank You, God, for using me to
show Your love to Your people.

Your beauty should come from within you—
the beauty of a gentle and quiet spirit.

1 Peter 3:4

What do you think it takes to be beautiful? Circle your answers below:

- flawless skin
- large eyes
- long eyelashes
- lots of makeup
- painted nails
- straight, white teeth
- long, flowy hair
- the latest style of clothes

Did you circle them all? You might have if you get your ideas of beauty from movies and magazines. But God has an entirely different perspective.

God intends all of His girls to be gorgeous, but not by buying the latest beauty products or wearing a certain style of jeans. In fact, He tells us in 1 Peter that we don't even need to bother with all that stuff because it only covers the surface. These things don't last, and they don't tell others who you really are. Real and true beauty only comes from God's Spirit living inside us.

True beauty is being nice to someone who's been mean to you or helping your brother clean his room. It's sticking up for a kid who has being bullied or helping to make peace between two friends who are arguing. In other words, it's the fruit of God's Spirit living inside you: love, joy, peace, patience, kindness, goodness, gentleness, faithfulness, and self-control! When we let go of our selfish wants

and let God's Spirit be our guide for living, God grows His beautiful fruit in our lives so that others can see and taste His goodness through the things we do and say.

PRayeR PoiNteR

I want to be God's kind of gorgeous. Holy Spirit, please help me grow in Your goodness!

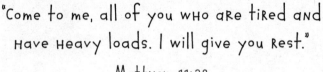

> "Come to me, all of you who are tired and have heavy loads. I will give you rest."
>
> Matthew 11:28

Have you ever stayed up really, really late or maybe even pulled an all-nighter at a lock-in? If so, circle the symptoms below that you saw and felt the next morning:

- tired eyes
- extreme tiredness
- grouchy attitude
- just feeling gross in general
- dry eyes
- unable to think or speak clearly

Sometimes an event seems like it's going to be so much fun that it's worth missing sleep for it, but our bodies eventually tell us a different story: *You need sleep more than you realize!* Sleep helps our bodies reset and restores all our cells to proper working order so that we have the energy to think and talk and be active.

The same is true for our spiritual lives. Sometimes we can get caught up doing our daily routine—going to school, doing our homework, playing sports, and then going to bed again—and we completely miss spending time with God. But taking time out of the busyness of the day to be with Jesus is like giving your body the good rest that it needs to recharge. Through God's Word and His

Spirit, He renews our minds and fuels us with the energy we need to follow Him throughout our busy days.

Circle a time of day below to spend time with God that best fits your schedule, and make sure you get your spiritual beauty rest today!

- when I wake up
- after breakfast
- at lunch
- after school
- at night before bed

PRAYER POINTER

Lord, thank You for offering me much-needed rest through spending time with You each day.

"Honor your father and your mother."

Exodus 20:12

Your parents have fed and clothed you since you were born. They were excited when you said your first words, they clapped when you crawled, and they took videos of you when you started to walk. In fact, they have celebrated you not only on your birthday but also when you acted in the school play, made a good grade on a test, competed in your favorite sport, and in all those wonderfully ordinary moments in between. Maybe, without your even realizing it, the people caring for you have made your life more beautiful than it ever would have been without them. And by their example, they've been showing you how to make other people's lives more lovely.

Today, let your parents know you notice and appreciate their love. Look for ways you can return the favor and add to the beauty of their day. Here are some ideas:

- Write a card listing all the reasons you appreciate them.
- Clean the kitchen or even the whole house.
- Plan a party for the family, inviting your siblings to help celebrate your mom and/or dad.
- Paint a picture of your favorite family memory.
- Make a banner to put on the front of your house telling everyone why your parents are so great.

Prayer Pointer

Thank You, Lord, for my parents. Help me honor them as I honor You in what I say and do.

Runway the Right Way

Help each other with your troubles. When you do this, you truly obey the law of Christ.

Galatians 6:2

Have you ever watched a fashion show? Typically, models walk down a runway displaying the designer garments they've been given to wear. Just like any show, a lot of prep work happens beforehand. The stage must be set, lighting fixed, wardrobes chosen, and makeup applied. Lots of different people need to do lots of different jobs before the show is ready to go on.

Just like all the people who make that runway show happen, everyone in your house has a role to play too. Each person has a job to do, whether it's your parents going to work, your siblings cleaning the dishes, or you taking care of the family pets. God says that one of the reasons He puts families together is so we can help carry each other's loads. We can make life better for each other, which brings glory to God and joy to our hearts. What can you do to help your family be better prepared for the day ahead? Circle your favorite ideas below or make up your own—then give them a try!

- Pray with them about their day before they leave.
- Help make breakfast and clean the kitchen.
- Tell them something encouraging about themselves.
- Give them a hug and tell them you love them.

Prayer Pointer

Lord, help me lighten the load of others around me.

I think about your orders and study your ways.

Psalm 119:15

When you need to prepare for a test, what do you need to do to succeed?

- Go play outside.
- Worry about it a lot.
- Get a friend to help you study.
- Go through your notes and memorize answers.

While you actually might do all of the above, going through your notes and memorizing the answers either alone or with a friend will help you best remember the material for the test. The same is true for learning God's Word. It's great to go to church and hear Bible lessons. It's also wise to read the Bible each day. But if you really want to remember what you've heard or read, you'll have to get serious and memorize it.

Memorizing verses with a friend or family member can help you learn the Scriptures and encourage you to keep learning them, but you can find ways to make it interesting on your own too. Have you ever checked out apps that help you learn new verses each day? Some use songs, puzzles, cues, and quizzes to make it fun. Or you could take a non-digital route: Get a recipe box and index cards with eight divider tabs. Write the name of each day of the week on seven of the tabs, then write "Monthly" on the eighth tab. Write out your favorite verses on the index cards and place

one behind each day-of-the-week tab. On Sunday, study the verse behind the Sunday tab—and so on for the rest of the week. When you memorize a verse, put the card behind the monthly tab, and write a new verse to replace the memorized one. Once a month, review the verses behind the monthly tab.

PRAYER POINTER

Father, help me remember Your Word all the days of my life.

Comfort each other and give each other strength, just as you are doing now.

1 Thessalonians 5:11

Have you ever wondered why there are so many greeting cards to choose from in some stores? Usually they are divided into sections: Birthday, Congratulations, Baby, Sympathy, and so on. When it comes time to pick the perfect one for your family member or friend, it can take a really long time to search through them all! You want to find one that has just the right words for the moment.

And that's often why we buy cards for people—because it can be hard to think of the right words on our own. But encouraging others is actually a kind of art we can learn through experience and practice. The more we practice writing and saying words to help others feel better, the better at it we become.

To become a great encourager, choose from the activities below, and put your art into practice today.

- Cut a large piece of cardstock paper in half. On each piece, paint a simple watercolor picture and write your favorite Bible verse above or below the picture. Then visit a local nursing home and hand out your pictures to the elderly patients, or give them to some of the older people at your church. Look the people in the eye, talk to them, and hug them.
- Write fun and encouraging messages on a bunch of colorful sticky notes. Then stick them in surprising places for your

parents or siblings to discover (like in the microwave or fridge, on the car steering wheel, or in a purse or wallet.).

- Write a letter to your pastor, teacher, or youth group leader to say thank you for all he or she does for other people. Be sure to mention how you have been helped in particular.

PRayeR PointeR

Jesus, give me words of encouragement so I can always build up others.

> "THOSE WHO WORK TO BRING PEACE ARE
> HAPPY. God will call tHEM His SONS."
>
> MatτHEW 5:9

Have you ever held two magnets together and felt the push or pull? If you put the two ends that repel each other together, you feel an invisible force pushing the two magnets apart—they just can't come together. But if you turn one of the magnets around, suddenly they "click" right together!

Relationships can be a lot like those magnets. If both you and another person each demand your own way (for example, "I should get to be on the computer first!"), you will fight and just end up hurting each other's feelings. No matter how hard you try to convince the other person you're right, the two of you just won't come together, like the wrong ends of those magnets.

However, Jesus can help *you* change. He can turn your heart away from wanting your own way to being willing to serve the other person. ("Go ahead. You can go first. I'll play next.") When we try to follow God and allow Him to change our hearts, we find that we fit in better with God's plan for peace, and we "click" with others around us.

PRayeR PoiNteR

Jesus, help me be willing to put other people's needs before my own so that I can be a peacemaker.

Out of the Box

God did not give us a spirit that
makes us afraid. He gave us a spirit of
power and love and self-control.

2 Timothy 1:7

Every day that you go to school, you follow the same routine. You know what to expect, and that's great—schedules and order make our world feel safer and easier to handle.

But God hasn't called us to feel comfortable all the time. Instead, He wants us to grow in our obedience and to trust in His Spirit, and sometimes that means getting out of our comfort zone. That can feel scary, but remember: God can make you brave! When we trust and follow God's lead, great things happen.

Consider the ideas below. Ask God if He would like you to put them into practice. Then ask for the power and bravery to obey!

- One day each week at lunch, invite someone new to sit with you and your friends. Be sure to make her feel welcome!
- Look for the quiet person who rarely talks in class or who doesn't really hang out with other kids. Strike up a conversation with her.
- In PE, choose kids who are usually picked last to be on your team.
- Start a prayer club. Invite people to meet before or after school, or during lunch, to pray with you.

Prayer Pointer

Lord, please make me brave enough to go where
You want me to go and tell others about You.

> "There are many people to harvest, but there are only a few workers to help harvest them."
>
> Matthew 9:37

When you think of the mission field, what comes to mind? Does it usually involve dirt roads, palm trees, and people who don't speak your language? For sure, there are some mission fields that look like that. But they can also look exactly like your own neighborhood because, guess what? Right where you live *is* a mission field! Isn't it exciting that you don't have to get on a plane to change people's lives? Just start right where you are, reaching out to those people you see every day but with whom you may not have had meaningful conversations yet.

Look at the list of activities below, and choose at least two that will help you connect with your neighbors and to show them God's love!

- Bake cookies with your mom or dad, put them in a cute container, and include a card that says, "God loves you, and I do too!" Together, take them to your neighbor's house, ring the doorbell, and, if you've never met them before, introduce yourself. Tell them you're glad they are in the neighborhood, and let them know you want to be of help if they ever need anything. Share that you are praying for the people in your neighborhood, and ask if they have any prayer requests. If they do, see if they'd let you say a short prayer with them before you leave.

- Offer to clean your neighbor's yard, rake their leaves, or take their garbage to the curb for free. When they ask why, tell them you love Jesus and want to serve His people just like He did.
- Get some friends together and launch a Neighborhood Backyard Bible Club. Meet once a week to pray together and work on projects to help others. Encourage everyone to bring a new friend each week.

PRAYER POINTER

Jesus, please use me to help my
neighbors know Your love better.

> The smoke from the incense went up from the angel's hand to God. It went up with the prayers of God's people.
>
> Revelation 8:4

D o you know what smells beautiful to God? Out of all the incredible scents He created in the world, the one He loves most is the sweet-smelling scent of the prayers of His people!

The Old Testament talks about people using incense—a mixture of fragrant spices and oils that are burned—when they worshipped God in the temple. In the book of Revelation, John describes prayers being kept in incense bowls and then rising up before God's throne, just like the burning incense in the temple. Prayer is a beautiful offering from us to God.

God loves our prayers because they connect us to Him. Prayer helps us realize how much we need God for everything and how able He is to meet our deepest needs.

So do you want to grow in beauty? Then grow a stronger prayer life. Use the ideas below to help you come closer to God and learn to pray about what matters most to Him.

- The book of Psalms is a collection of prayers and songs. Each day, choose a different psalm to read. Try to take the words of the psalm and turn it into your own prayer. For example, Psalm 23:1 says, "The Lord is my shepherd. I have everything I need." You might then pray, "Thank You, Lord, for being my Shepherd and for giving me all that I need."

- Pray for wisdom to know how and what to pray. Ask the Holy Spirit to lead your thoughts and words.
- Get a notebook with five subject tabs and label them with the words *Me*, *Family*, *Friends*, *Church*, and *World*. In each section, write specific prayer requests for that subject. Pray for them, and make a note of the date. When God answers your prayers, write that down too!

Prayer Pointer

Lord, prayer keeps me close to Your heart. Thank You for listening to me and leading me!

I thank God every time I remember you. And
I always pray for all of you with joy.

Philippians 1:3-4

You watch for it, and you count down the days until it arrives. Finally, it's time! It's your birthday, and you hope everyone else is as excited about it as you are. It's the one day when it seems okay for it to be truly all about you.

But you're not the only one who feels that way. Every kid in your class has the same hopes and wishes when their big day rolls around. So do the kids you sponsor through your church or local charity. So do parents and grandparents (whether they admit it or not). Simply put, birthdays are natural occasions to celebrate loved ones and let them know we're glad God put them on this earth. It's also an easy way for you to think about other people and their needs and to send a little love and encouragement their way.

Ask your mom or dad to help you make (or buy) a calendar. Then:

- Call or text your friends and family members and ask them when their birthdays are (if you don't already know). Write each name on the correct date on your calendar. Go ahead and get their mailing addresses while you're at it.
- Make or purchase a large stack of birthday cards. You could do chores around the house to earn money for the cards and stamps.

- About three to five days before each person's birthday, write a sweet note in a card, letting that person know how special he or she is to you and to God. Address the card, stamp it, and mail it. Your card will be a great reminder of your love and God's love—and that's the best birthday present around!
- Pray for each person on his or her birthday.

Prayer Pointer

Jesus, thank You for always remembering me.
Help me share that love with others.

> "ANYTHING you did foR aNY of my people HeRe, you also did foR me."

Matthew 25:40

Once, when Jesus had been teaching a large crowd for a long time, He said it was time for them to eat. The disciples planned to send everybody home for dinner, but Jesus said, "You feed them." They were confused! How could they feed so many people when they had practically no money or food? Then Jesus showed them a miracle. He took what little was there (just one young boy's lunch) and thanked God for it. Then He gave the food to the people—and thousands were able to eat all they wanted!

You can mirror Jesus' love for the poor and hungry by feeding them too. Ask your parents to help you find a food bank or soup kitchen where you can serve. When you go, do the following:

- Get to know the customers by name. Smile and tell them your name too.
- Don't just serve food—give lots of kindness too!
- Commit to coming back at a regular time.
- Sit and talk to the people, especially the kids. Find out about their families and their lives. Pray with them.
- Tell your friends about what you're doing, and invite them to join you.

PRayeR PointeR

Father, thank You for caring about the poor and needy. Please use me to show them Your love.

Deeds Day

We should show [our] love by what we do.
1 John 3:18

Whether you have been going to church your whole life or you are just starting to make church a regular part of your week, it's a place where you can enjoy youth group meetings, get-togethers with family and friends, and great worship time. So what can you do to give back to the place God is using to bless you so much? Take a look at the ideas below, and then talk to your pastor or other church leader. Ask which idea would be the biggest blessing for the church, or ask if there is another need you could fill. Then gather your friends and their families together to help you plan a day of service for the church. Let Deeds Day begin!

- Weed the grounds.
- Clean the pews or worship service area.
- Ask your pastor what prayer requests he has for himself and/ or the church. Agree to pray daily for those requests.
- Clean up the playground.
- Wash all the toys in the children's rooms.
- Hold a car wash or a yard sale to raise money for equipment the church needs or to support one of the church's mission projects.

Prayer Pointer

Thank You, God, for giving me my church family. Help me serve them back.

Share with God's people who need help.

Romans 12:13

Question: What do the following situations have in common?

- You found out that your friend's parent is having surgery this week.
- A family from church just brought home two new foster kids.
- Your neighbor recently lost a family member to an illness.
- The widow you know at church mentioned being lonely.

Answer: They are perfect opportunities to bring a meal to someone!

When interruptions happen—whether they are pleasant or unpleasant—life can get crazy. For the person who is having a difficult time, it can be really hard to cook and clean while trying to manage everything else that's going on. So when you step in to help out, they will remember that they're not alone. It will comfort them to know that people around them want to lighten their load however they can. Taking someone a meal is a beautiful—and tasty—way to share God's love and care with the people around you.

Here's what you can do:

- Ask your parents if they will help you cook and deliver a meal to the person who needs help. Even simple sandwiches delivered with a smile are a wonderful help.
- Contact the person you'd like to take a meal to and ask them what night you could bring dinner. Be sure to ask if anyone in his/her family has any allergies or food sensitivities that you should avoid.

- Plan and cook the meal. If possible, use disposable pans or containers so the person doesn't have to worry with washing or returning dishes.
- Be on time to deliver the meal, and be prepared to stay a few minutes so you can talk and pray together before you leave. If the person is alone and needs company, stay more than a few minutes!

Prayer Pointer

Jesus, You are my daily bread. Thank You for the chance to feed other people with Your love too.

God gave us the work of bringing
everyone into peace with Him.

2 Corinthians 5:18

When Adam and Eve disobeyed in the garden, more than just Paradise was lost. The connection between God and His people was broken. And the relationships between His people broke apart as well. But Jesus came to repair what sin tore apart. Through Jesus, we can be close to God and love other people the way we were meant to.

As God's kids, we are called to be *bridge-builders*. That means we are to be people who reach out to those who feel separated from God and from others. We can bridge that gap by bringing them close to Jesus. In fact, the Bible says that God considers reaching out to the hurting, such as widows and orphans, to be what real Christianity looks like.

So how can you be a bridge-builder? Think about the following ideas, and talk to your parents about ways you can help build bridges in your community with those who need it most.

- Contact a special needs ministry in a church and volunteer one Sunday a month. Choose one child who could use your help. Get to know that child and find out how you could help meet his or her needs.
- Get a list of the widows in your church. Call each one, introduce yourself, and ask them how you can best pray for any needs they have. Try to meet them in person, if you can.

- Reach out to the younger kids in your church. Get to know them, encourage them, and pray with them. Perhaps you and your friends could volunteer to help in their class once a month.

PRAYER POINTER

Jesus, please use me to love those who feel lost, different, or disconnected.

BEAUTIFULLY CLOTHED

E very day it's a fun challenge. I go to my closet, look through my clothes, and try to figure out which ones I want to put on that day for the right look. Sometimes I realize that what's there doesn't fit me anymore, has holes or stains, or just isn't my style anymore.

Well, strangely enough, choosing which clothes to wear doesn't just happen at my closet. It also happens in my heart. The Bible says our attitudes and thoughts are like pieces of clothing. God tells us to get rid of the stuff that doesn't fit us anymore even since we've become His children. In other words, now that we know how much we're loved and how special we are because of Jesus, we don't need to go around wearing old things like disobedience, bitterness, anger, gossip, or any of the other sins that used to be part of our lives. Even though situations may pop up that make us want to pull out our old bad habits, God gives us the power to say no to those old things and to say yes to—or to put on the new clothes of love, joy, peace, and kindness that Jesus offers.

In this next section, you'll find some practical examples of what I mean. You can decide which attitudes look like clothes from our  old sinful wardrobes (that need to be thrown away) and which are from the beautiful new wardrobe God has available for His kids (that we need to put on). Soon you'll have a good idea of how you can feel beautiful in God's clothes every day!

—Glory

Powerful Weakness

"WHEN you aRe weak, tHeN my
poweR is made peRfect iN you."

2 CoRiNtHiaNs 12:9

After her Sunday school lesson, Hope thought to herself, *Okay, I'm supposed to always obey my parents, love others, and answer with a kind word. Got it!* Confident that she was good enough and strong enough to do those things, Hope left class and got in the car to ride home with her family. Immediately, one of her brothers grabbed her video game that she'd left on the seat.

How do you think Hope will respond?

Like all God's kids, Hope has a choice to make. She can choose to serve herself or to serve God in the next few moments. It's a lot like choosing which outfit you are going to put on and show the world. Is she going to put on anger and selfishness, or instead is she going to throw those attitudes in the trash and put on patience, obedience, and love?

Read the two wardrobe options on the following page, and circle the wardrobe that shows God's glory best.

Wardrobe Option 1

"Give it back!" She scowled at her brother.

"But I got it first," he replied.

Then Hope's mother said, "Hope, honey, please let your brother play for a little while."

"No!" she argued. "It's my game, and he shouldn't have it!"

Wardrobe Option 2

Hope remembered her Sunday school teacher's lesson and knew she'd need help to obey. *God,* she prayed, *I want to do what's right, but I am weak on my own. Please give me strength to follow You.*

Hope was tempted to argue with her brother, but God's Spirit nudged her to be kind. "You can have it for now," she said to her brother, "but I'd like it back when we get home."

Which wardrobe above would *you* choose in this situation?

Prayer Pointer

God, I can never be good on my own. Please fill me with Your Spirit so that I can do what is right.

Fashioned for Love

> "But I tell you, love your enemies.
> Pray for those who hurt you."
>
> Matthew 5:44

Everyone at church was concerned. Outside, a large group of atheists (people who don't believe God is real) was picketing. One of the church members got angry and barged out of the church, waving her hands and yelling, "Go away! You and your stupid ideas aren't welcome here!" Some of the picketers yelled back.

Then a young, brave girl decided to take action. She got her youth group to help her load up some trays of donuts and juice that were supposed to be for Sunday school. Instead, they prayed for help and wisdom, then took the goodies outside to the picketers. As they handed out the juice and donuts, the kids smiled and told each person that God loved them and cared for them as they handed out the juice and donuts. After a while, the picketers got quiet. Eventually they all left—except for one man. He followed the kids back into the church, sat through the sermon, and gave his life to Jesus.

- Which church member was wearing an "old wardrobe"? What did she need to put on instead?
- What was the young, brave girl wearing? How did her "outfit" change the situation?
- Why is it so important to love others well, especially those who seem like our enemies?

Prayer Pointer

Jesus, clothe me with Your love so that I
can help others know You better.

Caught by Pride

Day 49

> God is against the proud, but He
> gives grace to the humble.
>
> James 4:6

Hope's dad planned a fishing trip for her and her brothers. "Everybody needs to pitch in so that we bring what we need," her dad said. The boys listened to their dad list what they needed to get, but Hope went into the garage, thinking she already knew what to do.

When they got to the lake, Hope realized she'd left her tackle box at home. She was still determined to catch the biggest fish, so instead of asking her dad for help, she took off and decided she would figure it all out on her own. After spending thirty minutes trying to find some bait, she finally went back. By the time she got there, her brothers had already landed two keeper-sized bass. Finally, Hope admitted that she wasn't the world's best fisherwoman, and she needed some help. Her dad was happy to give it.

- What do you call an attitude that says, *I don't need your help. I'm smart enough to do this on my own*?
- Read Philippians 2. What kind of attitude does God ask us to wear instead?
- Why do you think it's important to stay humble before God and others?

Prayer Pointer

God, I'm being foolish and full of pride whenever I think I'm better than others or that I can live without Your help. I need You for everything!

80

Godliness with contentment is great gain.

1 Timothy 6:6 NKJV

Glory was beside herself with excitement. Her grandparents had come into town to take her and a friend to the local fair. In a day filled with fun, they rode every ride, ate funnel cakes and candied apples, and even got to sit on the camel at the petting zoo. When it got dark, Grandmom and Granddad were exhausted. "We think it's time to go home now," they said. But Glory and her friend were still buzzing with energy.

Old Wardrobe: "Oh, come on, it's still early! We're not even tired yet!" Glory rattled off excitedly. "And there's one more section of the park we haven't seen! Plus, I really wanted to try to win a stuffed animal."

New Wardrobe: "Okay, Grandmom and Granddad. I bet you are tired—we've done so many incredible things! Thank you so much for taking us to the fair. It's been awesome!"

- How do you think Glory's "old wardrobe" words made her grandparents feel?
- Why is it so important to be content and thankful instead of always looking for something more?
- How would your attitude improve if you chose to be thankful and content with what you have instead of always wanting more?

Prayer Pointer

Father, thank You for filling my life with so many wonderful people and things. You are so good to me!

> We destroy every proud thing that raises itself against the knowledge of God.

2 Corinthians 10:5

Emma had been waiting all day to go to the pool with her mom, who had said they could go after she finished running errands. After hours had passed by and it was late in the day, her mom finally admitted, "I'm sorry, Emma. We'll have to go some other time. I'm having a dinner party tonight, and I just wasn't able to get everything together for it in time." Just as Emma felt her hopes evaporating, her mom added, "So I'm going to need your help cleaning up the kitchen and living room."

Old Wardrobe: Emma was furious. Now she not only had her plans canceled but her mom wanted her to help clean instead? "I'm not helping you clean anything since you didn't take me to the pool like you said you would!" Emma snapped, stomping off to her room to be alone.

New Wardrobe: Emma felt very frustrated and told her mom she was really disappointed. She prayed silently and asked God to help her with her attitude. Then she turned on some music and started putting away the dishes. After a while, her anger went away, and she began chatting with her mom about who was coming to the party.

- Could Emma keep from feeling upset when her plans were changed?
- What "new wardrobe" action did Emma take that helped her get rid of her anger and put on a servant's heart instead?
- How does choosing to obey God first have an impact on how we feel?

PRayeR PoiNteR

Lord, I don't ever need to try to get revenge or to get even. Help me choose what is good, even when I don't feel like it.

Getting to Give

Day 52

Do not be interested only in your own life, but be interested in the lives of others.

Philippians 2:4

It was Saturday, and Amanda was looking forward to going to the mall to get that outfit she'd been wanting. But Amanda's dad had other plans. "Honey, we have a family coming over who could use some encouragement," he explained. "The father has been out of work for a while, so I invited them over for the day so you could play with the kids while the grown-ups talk."

Old Wardrobe: Amanda crossed her arms. "I don't even know those people," she whined. "It's not my fault they have problems. I had plans today. We can help them some other time."

New Wardrobe: Amanda thought about how that family must feel. She realized that even though she really wanted that new outfit, she had plenty of clothes already. So she said, "Okay. Tell me the ages of the kids. I'll plan something really fun to do while they're here."

Attitudes at Work: Where in the old and new "wardrobes" do you see the following attitudes? Write the number of the attitude next to that part in the story.

1. generosity
2. selfishness
3. kindness
4. materialism (wanting more stuff)
5. creativity
6. compassion

Prayer Pointer

Jesus, You have said it's better to give than receive. Help me believe it and live it!

Mending Hope

TRust tHe LoRd witH all youR HeaRt. Don't
depend on youR own undeRstanding.

PRoveRbs 3:5

Hope was losing hope as she watched the doctor x-ray her arm. "I'm afraid it's broken in two places," he confirmed. "You're going to need to be in a cast for at least six weeks." Tears filled her eyes as she turned to her mom and said, "But I'm supposed to play in the state championships this weekend!"

Old WaRdRobe: "I can't believe God let this happen to me!" Hope cried. "Doesn't He know how important that game was to me?"

New WaRdRobe: Tears fell down Hope's face as she felt deep disappointment. Then she prayed for strength. "God, I don't know why this happened, but I know that You are in control. You keep Your promises, so I know this will somehow work out for my good."

Attitudes at WoRk: Where in the old and new "wardrobes" do you see the following attitudes? Write the number of the attitude next to that part in the story.

1. doubt
2. belief
3. depending on God
4. despair, or giving up hope
5. anger
6. trust
7. blaming God
8. faithfulness
9. unbelief

PRayeR PointeR

God, help me believe You are good even
when things don't go my way.

Dealing with Disappointment

Love is patient and kind. Love is not jealous.

1 CORINTHIANS 13:4

Glory had practiced countless hours to audition for the school play. Today, the cast list came out, and she discovered she'd been given a background part. However, her good friend Gracie—who has an incredible singing voice—had landed the lead role. A flood of emotions washed over Glory.

Old Wardrobe: Glory's disappointment quickly melted into anger, followed by jealousy. *I worked harder than anybody to get that part! And Gracie always gets whatever she wants.*

New Wardrobe: "Wow, that's disappointing," Glory admitted out loud. Then she remembered the verse she had read that morning about God directing her steps. *Well, Lord,* she prayed, *You must have other plans for me. Thanks for helping me do my best.* When she saw Gracie, she gave her a tight hug and said, "Congratulations! You'll be great."

Attitudes at Work: Where in the old and new "wardrobes" do you see the following attitudes? Write the number of the attitude next to that part in the story.

1. anger
2. love
3. understanding
4. resentment
5. wisdom
6. jealousy
7. obedience
8. blame

Prayer Pointer

God, help me trust You when I am disappointed and give thanks to You no matter what happens.

Letting Grudges Go

Love does not remember wrongs done against it.

1 Corinthians 13:5

Honor could hardly believe her eyes when Mandy raised her hand in youth group, showing that she wanted to become a Christian. Honor wasn't sure how she felt about it. Mandy had been mean to her all year long. Now it looked like Mandy was going to accept Jesus and join her youth group.

Old Wardrobe: *I bet it's just another trick to get attention,* Honor thought. *She'll just go back to her old ways. And if she thinks I'm going to forget everything she's done to me, then she's crazy!*

New Wardrobe: *Wow, Lord, You really amaze me,* Honor silently prayed. *Now would You work in my heart too? I'm going to need help forgiving Mandy. Help me love her like You do.* Then Honor got up and put her arm around Mandy while she prayed with the youth leader.

Attitudes at Work: Where in the old and new "wardrobes" do you see the following attitudes? Write the number of the attitude next to that part in the story.

1. resentment
2. trusting God
3. holding a grudge
4. believing the best
5. doubting God
6. hate
7. love
8. spite
9. forgiveness

Prayer Pointer

Father, help me forgive and love others—and
treat them as You have treated me.

> AN evil peRsoN causes tRouble. And a
> peRsoN wHo gossips Ruins fRiendsHips.
>
> PRoveRbs 16:28

F aith always looked forward to seeing her friends from youth group each Sunday. Today, their leader was late, so the girls were chatting about their week. "Did you hear what happened after school on Friday?" one of the girls asked. Then she continued, "I heard Olivia got in a fight with Sophia over that new girl who invited Sophia over..."

old WaRdRobe: "No, I didn't hear about that!" Faith said, totally interested in the story. "How bad did the fight get? Olivia can get pretty dramatic. I bet she's the one who started it."

New WaRdRobe: "No, I didn't hear about it and probably shouldn't either," Faith said. "I like both of those girls. Plus, God wants us to encourage each other—you know, be kind." Then Faith changed the subject by asking, "So how was your weekend?"

Attitudes at Work: Where in the old and new "wardrobes" do you see the following attitudes? Write the number of the attitude next to that part in the story.

1. kindness
2. tearing others down
3. gossip
4. seeking unity
5. causing others not to get along
6. faithfulness

PRayeR PoinTeR

Jesus, please help me to encourage others
with my words and to avoid gossip.

Pay Back or Bless Back?

Do not do wrong to a person to pay him back for doing wrong to you. . . . But ask God to bless that person.

1 Peter 3:9

Gracie knew that going to a new school wouldn't be easy, but she could hardly believe what happened one day. "Did you hear what Tara is saying about you?" Ava, one of Gracie's new friends, asked. "She's saying you're stuck-up and that people shouldn't talk to you." Tara was one of the popular girls, and Gracie became very worried.

Old Wardrobe: "*She's* the one who's stuck-up . . . and super snotty!" Gracie retorted. "She doesn't know who she's messing with. I can make life just as miserable for her."

New Wardrobe: "Well, I guess Tara just doesn't know me yet," Gracie answered. She silently prayed, "Lord, help me make good friends here, and help Tara see the truth." The next day, Gracie helped Tara pick up books she dropped. Tara still wasn't friendly, but Gracie said, "Hey, I can be quiet sometimes, but I'm not stuck-up. I'd really like to be friends with everyone here."

Attitudes at Work: Where in the old and new "wardrobes" do you see the following attitudes? Write the number of the attitude next to that part in the story.

1. anger
2. revenge
3. hate
4 depending on God
5. peacemaking
6. boldness

Prayer Pointer:

God, help me be kind to others, even
when they are not kind to me.

Get rid of all evil and all lying. Do not be a hypocrite.

1 Peter 2:1

Ava was on the computer when her dad walked into the room. There was a family rule about not chatting with friends online, which was what Ava was doing. When her dad came in, Ava closed the chat screen and pulled up her homework page. "What exactly have you been doing, Ava?" her father asked.

Old Wardrobe: "It's just my homework, see?" Ava said.

"Then what are those other tabs in the corner?" her dad asked.

"Oh, that was just some research I had to do," Ava lied.

New Wardrobe: "Well, I really was doing my homework earlier. But I was also talking with some friends online, which I shouldn't have done," she admitted.

Her dad said, "I appreciate your honesty. But you disobeyed our rules, and it's going to cost you privileges for the rest of today."

"Yeah . . . okay, Dad," she answered and stepped away from the computer.

Attitudes at Work: Where in the old and new "wardrobes" do you see the following attitudes? Write the number of the attitude next to that part in the story.

1. obedience   3. disobedience   5. wisdom
2. lying   4. honesty   6. rebellion

Prayer Pointer

Lord, whenever I feel myself sneaking, I know I'm in sin. Help me stay true to You and others.

Thinking Beauty

Think about the things that are true and honorable and right and pure and beautiful and respected.

Philippians 4:8

sabella had started gymnastics at a new gym, and she liked the music they played there. It had a cool beat that made workouts more fun. At home, she found the same station and turned it up loud in her room. After a while, her mom popped in. "Isabella, what are you listening to? Can you hear what that song is saying?" Isabella started really listening. Then she was embarrassed.

Old Wardrobe: "I don't listen to the words. I just like the sound," Isabella answered.

"But you're letting that trash fill your mind. You're even singing it!" her mom replied.

"Everybody listens to this," Amanda argued.

New Wardrobe: "Wow, I really wasn't paying attention to the words. They're pretty bad. I'll listen to something different," Amanda said.

"And I'll talk to your coach about switching the station at practice," her mom added.

Attitudes at Work: Where in the old and new "wardrobes" do you see the following attitudes? Write the number of the attitude next to that part in the story.

1. pleasing God   3. crude talk   5. rebellion
2. just doing what everyone else does   4. purity

Prayer Pointer

Jesus, help me think pure thoughts and choose entertainment that doesn't dishonor You.

> ONLY God is important, because He is
> the One who makes things grow.
>
> 1 CORINTHIANS 3:7

As a new Christian, Gracie was getting tips from the youth group girls and from church sermons about how Christians behave. She also learned about quiet time, prayer, journaling, memorizing Scripture . . . the list went on and on! It all seemed pretty overwhelming.

Old Wardrobe: *Maybe I need a checklist to make sure I do everything good Christians are supposed to do,* Gracie thought. *Plus, I'll fit in better with the girls who are doing everything right.*

New Wardrobe: *Lord, help! I'm overwhelmed by all the dos and don'ts I'm hearing,* Gracie prayed. *These ideas are good, but they don't make me more worthy of Your love. I'm completely accepted and loved by You because of what Jesus did for me, not what I do for You.*

Attitudes at Work: Where in the old and new "wardrobes" do you see the following attitudes? Write the number of the attitude next to that part in the story.

1. loving God
2. self-righteousness
3. depending on yourself
4. pleasing God
5. depending on God
6. pleasing people
7. accepting God's help and grace

Prayer Pointer

Jesus, thank You that I don't have to earn Your love or approval. You give it freely to everyone who trusts in You!

Going for Glory

God, you are supreme over the skies.
Let your glory be over all the earth.

Psalm 108:5

Glory was thrilled. She had just created bathing suit designs that she thought were not only super stylish but also modest. So she invited all her friends over to see her designs. To her delight, her friends were amazed.

"These are incredible!" Faith said.

"How'd you come up with such creative designs?" Honor asked.

Old Wardrobe: "Well, I'm just good at fashion, you know," Glory answered proudly. "I've been working really hard so I can be famous someday. I want my name to be the brand everybody buys."

New Wardrobe: "Thanks, guys! I'm super excited about them too," Glory answered. "You know, I pray all the time for God to give me creative ideas to help others, and I think He's done just that!"

"He sure did!" Honor agreed. "It would be so cool for girls to have something this modest and stylish to wear!"

Attitudes at Work: Where in the old and new "wardrobes" do you see the following attitudes? Write the number of the attitude next to that part in the story.

1. giving glory to God
2. pride
3. trusting yourself
4. trusting God
5. stealing God's glory
6. using your talents for God

Prayer Pointer

Jesus, let my life be a beautiful reflection
of Your glory in all that I say and do.

KINGDOM FITNESS

am all about games and fitness, so I volunteered to create this next section to add a fun and challenging twist to all this girl-ishness we have going on here! I've come up with some games to help you remember what Scripture says about beauty and our bodies and to help you look at your own life to see where these truths either fit or flop.

I think games are a great way to help us move from just reading and thinking to actively living out what God is teaching us.

To start, design your own calendar or print a blank one for the coming month. Then write in things you can do to add beauty to someone's life. Hope you have a ball!

—Hope

> Let us think about each other and help each other to show love and do good deeds.
>
> Hebrews 10:24

Want to be beautiful? Don't pull out the makeup just yet. Instead, think about the most beautiful, selfless things your mom or dad, or maybe a sibling or friend, has ever done for you. Aren't those moments worth a million times more than great hair or clothes?

In this exercise, you get to spend some time being beautiful—or at least planning for it. We've given you some ideas throughout the month, but fill in the remaining days with your own ideas for adding beauty to someone's life. Don't worry, you can repeat your favorite ideas! Then put your "beautiful" plan into practice.

- Give your mom a back massage.
- Write an encouraging note to your teacher.
- Say something encouraging to your sister or brother.
- Clean out the car without being asked.
- Call or text someone who needs a friend.
- Bring a flower to your Sunday school teacher.
- Take cookies to your neighbors.
- Make breakfast or coffee for your dad in the morning.

Prayer Pointer

God, show me how I can share Your love
with the people in my life today.

If you eat, or if you drink, or if you do anything, do everything for the glory of God.

1 Corinthians 10:31

Your physical body is a temple for God's Holy Spirit. So it's a no-brainer that you need to take care of it. But *knowing* what's good and actually *doing* it aren't always the same thing. Take this quiz to find your level of kingdom fitness.

1. Your friends started a game of soccer outside while you're in the middle of playing a video game you just don't want to quit. You:

   a. don't hear them laughing and kicking the ball because you're so engrossed in the game.
   b. hope they'll still be out there later when you finish this level.
   c. save your progress and join your friends right away.

2. You've just come home from school, and you're hungry. You look in the pantry and choose:

   a. your favorite bag of potato chips, and then you head for the sofa to watch TV.
   b. an apple and a bag of granola, and then you head for the sofa.
   c. an apple and a bag of granola, and then you head outside for a bike ride after your snack.

3. On average, you tend to exercise:

    a. only in your dreams.

    b. every now and then.

    c. on a consistent basis.

4. When you exercise or play a sport, you:

    a. consider watching other people exercise good enough.

    b. start off with enthusiasm, but often lose steam.

    c. work with all your might until the time is up.

If you answered mostly As, your fitness is totally flat. It's time to get up, out, and moving toward a healthier you. If you answered mostly Bs, your fitness is fair. Moderation is good, but push yourself a little more to achieve greater fitness. If you answered mostly Cs, congratulations! Your temple should be fit for whatever adventure God has in store!

PRayeR PoiNteR

God, help me to take good care of this body You've given me so I can be ready for whatever you have planned for me.

Think Again

> Listen, my child, and be wise. Keep
> your mind on what is right.
>
> Proverbs 23:19

God's Word says that what we think has the power to control what we do. The question is, do you know and believe God's truth? Take this simple true-or-false quiz to see if your thoughts about God match up with His Word.

1. T F Compared to some other people, I'm actually a pretty good person.
2. T F Sin is a thing of the past. Because of Jesus, God doesn't care about it anymore.
3. T F God will like me more if I work hard to obey Him.
4. T F God will get angry with me if I keep making the same mistake (or sin) over and over again.
5. T F If I sin too much, I can lose my salvation and won't get to go to heaven.

So what do you think? Did you answer True for any of the above? If so, you are missing some vital truths about God's love for you. Every statement above is false!

If you have put your faith in Jesus to save you, here's the truth:

- All people are sinners, equally deserving God's anger and punishment. Without Jesus, you have no hope of heaven (John 14:6; Romans 3:23).
- God still hates sin because He is still holy. Apart from Jesus, you would have to pay for your own sin, which means punishment forever! Jesus, however, not only takes away

your sin, He also gives you credit for His perfect record! Because of what Jesus did for you, even when you sin, God's love for you doesn't change or end (John 3:16–17; Romans 6:23).

- God's anger toward your sin ended when you decided to follow Jesus. God forgives you every time (2 Peter 3:9; 1 John 1:9).
- Once you are adopted into God's family through faith in Jesus, nothing can separate you from God's love (Romans 8:38–39; John 1:12).

Prayer Pointer

Jesus, thank You for paying for my sins so that I can enjoy friendship with God forever!

> THere is a RigHt time for everytHing.
> Everytning on eartH Has its special season.
>
> Ecclesiastes 3:1

God says that we need to make the most of our time here on earth, spending it on what matters most. But life happens so fast, we often don't even think about what we are doing with our time. So take a little time now to think about your time—and how well you're spending it.

1. When I come home from school, I typically:

   _____

2. Whenever I have to wait in a doctor's office, in the car, at restaurants, or wherever, I usually spend the time:

   _____

3. Really, the most important things that I can do in life are:

   _____

4. The amount of time I spend each day doing the things I just listed above is:

   _____

5. In light of what I believe is important, here are practical ways I could make better use of my time:

   a. in the morning:

   _____

   _____

b. at home:

_____

_____

c. at school:

_____

_____

d. at church:

_____

_____

e. in the evening:

_____

_____

f. on weekends:

_____

_____

g. to fit in exercise:

_____

_____

h. to limit screen time:

_____

_____

PRayeR PoiNteR

God, please keep me from wasting time on
what doesn't really matter, and help me use
the time You have given me for good.

> Come to me and listen. Listen
> to me so you may live.
>
> Isaiah 55:3

Isn't technology awesome? We can get all sorts of information, play endless games, watch videos, and text people—all with a computer, tablet, or phone. But if we don't watch it, we can lose the beauty of real-life relationships with people and with God when our technology starts to take over.

So has technology taken over your life, or do you have control over this high-tech temptation? Take this quiz to find out.

1. T F I have heard my parents complain about how often I'm on the computer/phone.
2. T F I find it very hard to stop playing and/or texting when it's time to do homework.
3. T F I often forget to look up from my device when someone is talking to me.
4. T F I feel uncomfortable when I don't have my device with me.
5. T F I sometimes look up things or click on tabs that might not be good.
6. T F I like to use earphones to keep my world to myself and keep other people out.
7. T F I often lose track of time when I'm on my device.
8. T F I check my device for new information and messages first thing every morning.

9. T F I often try to get on my device even after I'm supposed to be in bed.
10. T F I get snappy whenever my parents ask me to turn it off.

If you answered False to all of these, then congratulations! You are a tech master and are able to control your time with technology. If you answered True to any of the above, ask God to help you take back your time and turn your focus to Him and the people He's placed in your life.

Prayer Pointer

Jesus, help me to focus on You and to do the things
You want instead of focusing on a screen.

Gifted

We all have different gifts. Each gift came because of the grace that God gave us.

Romans 12:6

Did you know that God gives each of His kids a special gift to use for His kingdom? They may not be the kinds of gifts you open at birthday parties, but they are huge blessings to everyone when you open and use the gifts God has given you.

Read the gifts and their descriptions below. Then draw a square (think of it as a gift box) around the gift that best describes you. Ask God to help you use it to grow His kingdom!

1. You can easily turn an ordinary conversation into a talk about Jesus. People open up to you, and you're able to share the gospel with them and lead them to Christ.
2. You have a tender heart for those who've made mistakes, and you're willing to give others a second chance. You want to help them find God's forgiveness and love.
3. You're able to stand in front of others and tell them about what you've learned from the Bible (for example, leading little kids in Sunday school).
4. Whenever you are given money, you immediately begin to think about who needs it the most, and you find much joy in giving it to the people who do.
5. You often help people see the good in themselves and in their lives and to find their hope in Jesus.

6. You have a sharp sense of what is right or wrong based on knowing the Scriptures and listening to God's Spirit.

7. You get a deep pleasure from helping others—without needing recognition or attention.

- gift of generosity (giving)
- gift of teaching
- gift of discernment (knowing right and wrong)
- gift of service
- gift of evangelism (sharing the good news of Jesus)
- gift of mercy (forgiving)
- gift of encouragement

PRayeR PoiNteR

God, help me to use the gifts you have given me to tell the world about You.

Answers: 1. evangelism; 2. mercy; 3. teaching; 4. generosity;
5. encouragement; 6. discernment; 7. service

LoRd, you Have examined me.
You kNow all about me.

Psalm 139:1

Did you know that even before God made the world, *you* were on His mind? Incredible, right? Well, not only did He think about you, He also planned every single part of you—from the top of your head down to your itty bitty toes. God designed you to reflect His glory in a unique way that only you can.

Read Psalm 139 and learn just how special God thinks you are. Then fill in the blanks to the verses below (use the *International Children's Bible* translation), and find the words in the word search.

ACRoss

1. God knows my _____ before I think them.

2. God's knowledge about me is more than I can _____ _____.

3. Where can I go to get away from your Spirit? _____ _____.

4. You promise to hold me with Your _____ _____.

DowN

1. God _____ me in my mother's body.

2. God says His work in me is amazing and _____ _____.

3. God says all my days were _____ for me.

4. If I tried to count all the times God thinks about me, they would outnumber the _____ .

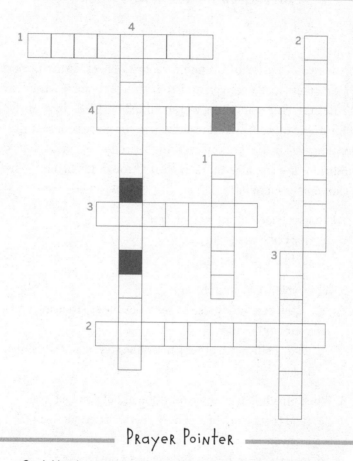

───────── Prayer Pointer ─────────

God, You know everything about me—the good and the bad—and You promise to love me forever. Thank You!

Answers: Across—1. thoughts; 2. understand; 3. nowhere; 4. right hand
Down—1. formed; 2. wonderful; 3. planned; 4. grains of sand

LoRd God, you aRe my Hope. I Have
tRusted you siNce I was youNg.

Psalm 71:5

H ave you ever been through a security check at the airport?
Scanners look over you and your things to make sure you're
not carrying something you shouldn't be. Well, this quiz isn't
that kind of scanner. It's a test to see where you place your security—
or confidence—in life. Are you carrying attitudes and ideas that you
shouldn't, or are you able to freely walk through life being the person God made you to be?

1. When you look in the mirror, you:
    a. don't like what you see.
    b. do like what you see.

2. When you are at church, you:
    a. watch everybody else to see what they're wearing and if
       your clothes fit in.
    b. enjoy being with other Christians so you can worship
       together.

3. When an adult asks you a question about yourself, you:
    a. tend to look down and only give short or one-word
       answers.
    b. look them in the eye and answer honestly and
       thoroughly.

4. When your pastor says, "God loves you," you:
    a. think it applies to everyone else except you.
    b. feel grateful and love God back.

5. When you see a new girl at school, you:
   a. avoid talking to her because she might not like you.
   b. go over and talk to her so that she'll feel better about the
      new school.

If you answered mostly As, then you're carrying extra baggage that you can throw away. God wants you to feel good about yourself and what you have to offer the world. Always remember that God lives inside you and will help you be the person He created you to be. If you answered mostly Bs, you've passed with flying colors. You understand that God not only loves you, but He likes you—a fact that makes you beautifully confident in Him.

Prayer Pointer

God, help me to see that all those wonderful promises in Your Word aren't just for other people—they're for me too!

"I Have called you by Name, and you aRe miNe."

Isaiah 43:1

Did you know that you have more names than just the one your parents gave you? God thinks you're so special, He uses all kinds of names to let you know who you are to Him. Each name gives you a glimpse of God's great love for you and for each one of us.

But just like the letters below are mixed up, our minds often mix up God's message of love. We begin to think we need to perform really well or be supergood all the time in order for Him to love us. But that kind of thinking is more scrambled than these words! God's love for us is steady and true because Jesus makes us right with God forever.

Unscramble the words below and understand just how deeply God cares for you—and always will!

SCHONE _____ 1 Peter 2:9

AYPHP _____ Psalm 32:1

ASDVE _____ Psalm 107:2

YHLO _____ Isaiah 62:12

NODLERWFU _____ Psalm 139:14

IEMN _____ Isaiah 43:1

IHS HICLREND _____ Ephesians 1:5

LEDOV NOE _____ Deuteronomy 33:12

INFRGVEO _____ Romans 4:7

EMAD EWN _____ 2 Corinthians 5:17

WTESE LSELM _____ 2 Corinthians 2:15

EBALUIFUT _____ Song of Songs 4:7

RSECIPOU _____ Isaiah 43:4

HODNORE _____ Isaiah 43:4

PRAYER POINTER

Father, thank You for Your amazing love.
You make me beautiful to You!

Answers: chosen, happy, saved, holy, wonderful, Mine, His children, loved
one, forgiven, made new, sweet smell, beautiful, precious, honored

CREATIVE BEAUTY

Introduction to Creative Beauty

In some ways I'm a city girl—kind of like Glory—because I love the straight lines and modern feel of the buildings and the busy, fast-paced lifestyle. But I have this other side too, the more secret part of me that loves to take long walks in the woods—or really anywhere out in nature. I'm fascinated by the many things God has made! I look at all the designs in plant leaves and spider webs, and I'm amazed. I'm fascinated with the way birds build their nests and with the way bees pollinate our world and keep things growing and living.

God's world is incredible . . . because *He* is brilliant! Nature reminds me that God is not boring or predictable. Instead, He is incredibly alive and full of wonder and surprises. He didn't make the world dull by just using all one color or shape either. He made it beautiful, complicated, totally out of the box, and more wonderful than I could have ever dreamed.

Nature helps me see *myself* better too, and realize that I don't have to look or be a certain way to be beautiful. God used His beautiful creativity to design me just the way I am, right this minute! I am unique in His creation. There's only one of me! And I bring a different kind of beauty to this wonderful world He has made. And guess what? You do too.

You are God's unique gift to this earth and to heaven. This section will help you celebrate God's creativity in and through you as an important part of His amazing world.

—Gracie

Plant Power

*My teaching will drop like rain. . . . [My words]
will pour down like rain on young plants.*

Deuteronomy 32:2

D o you know something spectacular is happening right now, right outside your front door? In fact, it's happening all around the world. And it's something that should help you breathe a little easier. Plants are making oxygen, and they're using sunlight to do it.

From the tiniest shoot to the tallest pine tree, plants are uniquely equipped with cells inside that act like food factories. As their leaves take in carbon dioxide from the air, they also use energy from sunlight, water, and soil nutrients to (amazingly) make a sugar called glucose. The plants use the glucose to feed themselves and grow. The most awesome part is that when plants create glucose, they release oxygen into the air, giving humans and animals the fresh air we breathe!

If you just look at a plant, you'd have no idea that all that cool stuff is happening inside. And the same is true for you! God is doing supernatural work inside you through the power of His Spirit. Just as plants soak up sunlight for energy, you can soak up spiritual energy by keeping your heart turned toward Jesus. That energy will help you do what's right—even when you might not want to or think you can. God provides everything you need for your faith to grow strong and healthy!

Prayer Pointer

Jesus, thank You for filling me with Your
energy so that I can live for You!

> We are His workmanship, created in
> Christ Jesus for good works.
>
> Ephesians 2:10 NKJV

Imagine if you had a superwide head with a long, pointed nose. Now add large lumps all over your body and huge fins. Top it off with almost fluorescent red lips. What would you be—other than horrifying? You'd be a red-lipped batfish!

At first the batfish may seem to have gotten a raw deal at creation. Not only does it look strange, but this fish can't even really swim. It just walks on the ocean floor using its pectoral fins.

But God, of course, had a reason for the way He made the batfish. Its strange dorsal fin sticks out like a fishing rod and lures in prey for an easy dinner. Those awkward walking fins keep it low to the ocean floor, making it harder to be seen and eaten by other creatures. And its bright-red lips help it attract other batfish. All its oddities actually protect and help the red-lipped batfish.

Aren't you glad you aren't a red-lipped batfish? Even so, you may have some features you wish you didn't. Just remember that God didn't make a mistake in your design. Your unique features fit in perfectly with His plan for your life—which God promises is a good plan. So trust Him! Be brave! Be the unique person God made you to be.

Prayer Pointer

God, help me appreciate Your creativity in my
design, and use me for Your kingdom.

Moonlight Madness

> He gave us light by letting us know the glory of God that is in the face of Christ.
>
> 2 Corinthians 4:6

If you're watching at just the right time of night, in just the right place along the beach, you can witness a marching miracle. Hundreds of baby sea turtles, newly hatched from eggs buried beneath the sand, poke through to their new world above and start their quest for the ocean. Using paddle-like flippers to push toward the sea, they seem to be born knowing exactly where to go.

Baby sea turtles have a problem though. Instinct tells them to head toward the light, which is a wonderful GPS feature when the moon is full and bright. But sometimes they hatch near people's homes and where streetlights give off a bright glow that looks a lot like the moon to a baby turtle. Confused, the turtles flip and flop onto busy streets instead of into the sea—a sad and tragic mistake.

In some ways, we're a lot like those turtles. We find ourselves drawn to the fake beauty of sinful things—just as those baby turtles are drawn to the fake "moon" of the streetlights. We can get confused and dazzled by the very things that can hurt us the most. God tells us to fix our eyes on Him and His perfect light. He'll always lead us to where we need to be.

Prayer Pointer

God, Your Word is a light for my path.
Thank You for leading me to life!

> "I will give you hidden riches. I will do
> this so you will know I am the Lord."

Isaiah 45:3

For years, there was something secret hidden underneath a mountain in Chihuahua, Mexico. This range of similar-looking, tall peaks was formed long ago through volcanic activity. Can you guess what excavators found one thousand feet below the surface of one of those mountains? An incredibly huge *crystal cave*. Imagine how surprised they were when they dug into the cave, pumped out the water, and discovered giant crystals, some as large as thirty-six feet long, sticking out in all directions from the cave walls . . . which were also covered in crystals! It was like discovering a crystal palace that had been growing for years, unseen until that moment. Who knew such beauty could grow so far below the surface?

God did—that's who. And the crystal cave is a beautiful reminder to us that what we see on the outside doesn't always give us the full picture. God wants us to dig deeper into people's lives—beyond outward appearances—and look for the hidden treasures of character and God's Spirit that may be growing there. God is doing a beautiful work in each believer's heart, and we don't want to miss the miracle because we're too distracted by what we see on the surface.

Prayer Pointer

God, help me see the beauty of Your life and Your
love in the believers You've placed around me.

An Egg-cellent Idea

No one has ever imagined what God has prepared for those who love Him.

1 Corinthians 2:9

Can you imagine a world without chicken eggs? Well, I guess at first you could. But then you'd start missing your scrambled egg breakfast. Cakes would go flat, and cookies would be thin and hard. Before long, chickens would disappear from the face of the earth! In the United States alone, more than 75 billion eggs are laid each year. They're not only a staple for all kinds of baking but also a good source of protein, choline for better brain development, and lutein for improved eyesight. It's amazing that those oval shells filled with goopy stuff have so much to offer!

The egg does something else too. It reminds us that God is very capable of creating something powerfully important inside a fragile shell, just like He does with us. Though our lives might seem small and even a little messy like the inside of an egg, God has created us perfectly to house His Spirit and to enrich the world around us with divine flavor.

So don't be so hard on yourself, trying to figure out what God could possibly do with you. Just look at the egg and remember that God is cooking up an incredible recipe for your life that will give the world a wonderful taste of His goodness and love.

Prayer Pointer

Father, just like You do with an egg, You turn my messy life into an amazing masterpiece!

Some people think they are doing what's right.
But what they are doing will really kill them.

PROVERBS 14:12

Don't polar bears look cute and cuddly on camera, sliding down snowbanks and playfully romping with their even cuter little cubs? Their coat of white fur not only protects them from the freezing cold temperatures of the Arctic where they live but also camouflages them in their icy surroundings so they can sneak up on unsuspecting seals—their favorite meal. Weighing up to 2,200 pounds each, polar bears have slightly webbed paws that help them paddle through the chilly waters for many miles in search of food.

But as soft and cuddly as polar bears may appear, humans who live near them know to keep their distance. Think about it: if polar bears can eat seals, walruses, and even whales, what would they likely do to people? *Exactly!*

Just like a polar bear, sin can seem harmless. Telling that lie to get out of trouble or sharing that bit of gossip might seem like a good idea—even innocent—at first. But cuddling up to a polar bear is dangerous, and so is sin. It can tear your soul to pieces, even though it looks so attractive from the outside. We need to distance ourselves from whatever tempts us to disobey God. Remember just because something looks harmless doesn't mean it is.

Prayer Pointer

Jesus, help me stay away from sinful
choices that can hurt me.

A Cut Above

> "THey sHall be Mine," says tHe LoRD of Hosts,
> "on tHe day tHat I make tHem My jewels."
>
> Malachi 3:17 N KJ V

Have you ever visited a jewelry store? Glass cases are filled with all different kinds of gems, each one specially cut and set in rings, earrings, bracelets, and necklaces to add beauty and color to the person who gets to wear them. Gemstones aren't a new trend either. Since almost the beginning of time, people have recognized certain gems—like diamonds, rubies, emeralds, and sapphires—as rare and precious. Though they come out of the rock and soil looking rough and cloudy, the special gems are cut just the right way to reveal the incredible beauty and shine from within.

Did you know that God views you as a precious jewel? Though you may not always see the beauty of your soul, God does. He has formed you and filled you with His own Spirit to give you a kind of rare shine that makes your life sparkle with His light and love. Just as precious gems must be cut to reveal the deepest beauty, so God works through the difficult times and the hurt and pain in your life to shape your character. Trust Him. God is using every moment in your life—even the toughest ones—to transform you into a beautiful gem who shines for Him.

PRayeR PointeR

Thank You, Jesus, for making me valuable
and beautiful to You and Your world.

> The teaching about the cross seems foolish
> to those who are lost. But to us who are
> being saved it is the power of God.
>
> 1 Corinthians 1:18

Lemurs are beautiful, ring-tailed primates from Madagascar known for their good looks, lively antics, and leaping abilities. But what lemur lovers may not know is how they smell. Male lemurs use scent glands to coat their tails with a pungent and powerful secretion to make them more attractive. Then they wave their tails in the air, hoping to lure a female lemur. Though to us the scent is terrible, the female lemur thinks it's terrific! The male with the strongest scent usually wins the girl.

God says that our lives and the message of Jesus have a similar effect in our world when it comes to telling people about Jesus. For those people still fighting God, who don't want to live their lives following Him, they think the message of the gospel stinks! But Jesus says that when we share the good news with others, it's a fragrant scent to Him—like perfume. For those people who are ready to hear about Jesus, it's a sweet scent too. We don't need to be afraid of how people may react when we share God's love. Instead, we can be confident that we're filling the world with the kind of fragrance that will lead God's people to Him.

Prayer Pointer

God, Your plan of salvation is a beautiful message
of hope that I want to share with others.

> We capture every thought and make
> it give up and obey Christ.
>
> 2 Corinthians 10:5

What are you doing right now? Okay, reading, for sure. But you are also thinking. So think about this: every day, approximately seventy thousand thoughts go through your mind! That number might not seem so big if you consider that your brain is made up of more than one hundred *billion* neurons—and that each one of those neurons has up to ten thousand synapses that help connect the neurons to each other. Add to that more than one hundred thousand miles of blood vessels that bring each of those neurons the oxygen and nutrients it needs to live and thrive. Just sitting there thinking, your brain produces enough physical energy to light up a light bulb. Wow!

With so much thinking going on, we need to make certain the thoughts we have are right and true! Beautiful thoughts lead to beautiful actions, but wrong and ugly thoughts lead to—you guessed it—wrong and ugly actions. God says that we can transform our minds (or change our way of thinking) by learning His Word and obeying what He says. Whenever we start thinking the wrong way, we actually need to fight it with God's truth and make our thoughts line up with what God says. When we do, our actions will show that we love God with our hearts, souls, and minds!

Prayer Pointer

Lord, help me to think about You and
stay in the truth of Your Word.

> Some trust in chariots, others in horses.
> But we trust the Lord our God.
>
> Psalm 20:7

Can you imagine sleeping while standing up? If you were a horse, you could! It's just one fascinating fact about these beautiful creatures that have helped humans since people first tamed them more than five thousand years ago. From the very beginning, people have recognized not only horses' beauty but also their power and speed as well. Able to run shortly after birth, young horses can grow to reach galloping speeds of over twenty-seven miles per hour. The fastest horse was clocked at fifty-five miles per hour.

Armies once used horses to carry their troops and supplies into battle. In fact, nations often measured their military strength by how many horses and chariots they had. However, God reminded His people over and over again in Scripture not to measure their strength by their possessions. Instead, He wanted them to look up to the only source of real hope and power—God Himself. As Creator of all the millions of horses on the earth today (along with everything else in the entire universe), God is our most powerful resource in life, especially in times of trouble.

Whenever you need help, let the horse's beauty and strength remind you of the One who made it and who invites you to come to Him for all you need.

—————— Prayer Pointer ——————

God, my help comes from You alone. Thank
You for being everything I need.

Light of the World

> "You are the light that gives
> light to the world."
>
> Matthew 5:14

H ave you ever wondered why sunrises and sunsets are so beautiful? Given the right combination of clouds on the horizon, blue skies erupt into flaming colors of red, orange, yellow, and even pink. So what makes the change happen? Light. Yep, the same sunlight that made the sky look blue can make it appear as all those other colors too. Sunlight contains all the color wavelengths, but different conditions in the atmosphere can absorb certain colors, leaving the remaining color wavelengths of light to reach our eyes. For instance, when the sun is low on the horizon, light waves have to travel farther to reach our eyes. The shorter blue waves get scattered and lost, while the longer wavelengths of red and yellow reach our eyes. Rain droplets in the clouds brighten the colors, creating a palette to display God's beautiful handiwork.

Jesus says God's kids are the light of the world. We don't create the light, but we channel it into its beautiful colors when we share our lunch with the kid who forgot his, take cookies to the firemen and thank them for protecting us, pray for the friend who is hurting, or tell someone how much Jesus loves them. Every day is a new day to paint the world with the colors of God's love.

Prayer Pointer

Lord, let Your light shine through me in the
most colorful and beautiful ways.

Don't make friends with someone
who easily gets angry. . . . If you do,
you may learn to be like him.

PROVERBS 22:24-25

ave you ever met someone who seemed nice at first, only to find out she had a really mean, angry side? In the animal world, she might be like the honey badger—the weasel-like creature with a strong love of honey (and every other kind of food), often considered to be one of the most fearless and ferocious animals around.

The honey badger often steals other animals' burrows and is famous for picking fights with any creature that crosses its path. Often the honey badger wins these fights because of its thick, rubbery skin and exceptionally strong teeth and jaws. And when it's frightened, it lets out one big stink bomb from the glands near its tail, very similar to a skunk.

Needless to say, honey badgers deserve some respect, but also some distance. The same is true for people who just like to pick fights with others. You will recognize them by how much they gossip or by their habit of insulting you or others to make themselves look better. It's good to pray for them and to answer them with love and wisdom whenever they approach, but don't try to be their best friend. Instead, look for others who love God and will help you move closer to Him.

Prayer Pointer

God, please help me choose friends
wisely and to pray for those who don't know You.

Oh, taste and see that the LORD is good;
Blessed is the man who trusts in Him!

Psalm 34:8 N K J V

What's your favorite flavor of ice cream? Now imagine if that were the only flavor there was in the whole world. Pretty soon you'd be sick of that flavor, right? Isn't it awesome that God created food with so many different textures and tastes?

How does our experience of taste even happen? It all starts with your saliva, which breaks down whatever food you're chewing. Then tiny hairs (called microvilli) on the ten thousand taste buds on your tongue send messages to your brain about what's washing over them. At the same time, special receptors in the top part of your nose send messages to the brain about what it smells you chewing. Then your brain combines the messages from the mouth and nose to give you the full sensation of the flavor—salty, sweet, sour, or bitter—of the food you're eating.

Why do you think God packs our world with so much flavor? Because it points us to how sweet and wonderful He is! God invites us to use all of our senses—seeing, smelling, tasting, hearing, touching—to put together the full flavor of His amazing creativity, kindness, power, and goodness. The next time you taste a flavor you love, thank God and think about how His love is even better!

Prayer Pointer

God, You are so good to me. Thank You for
yummy foods and a life filled with Your love!

Do not be shaped by this world. Instead be changed within by a new way of thinking.

Romans 12:2

What color is the cuttlefish? Whatever answer you give, you could be right, depending on the day and the surroundings of that particular creature. God designed the cuttlefish to protect itself by changing its colors to match its surroundings, also known as *camouflaging*. Cuttlefish skin is filled with *chromatophores*, which are special cells that each house a different color. When a cuttlefish wants to camouflage itself, it tightens the small muscles surrounding certain chromatophores while relaxing others. As the cells are squeezed, the color rises to the surface of the skin, making the cuttlefish's color change and form brilliant patterns. What an amazingly colorful and creative way to ward off attackers!

God's people, however, don't need these special abilities. God tells us not to blend in with the world around us, because the world isn't following Him. In fact, the more we are following Jesus, the less we will look like everybody else. And that's okay! People will see a difference in the way we love and care for others. They will hear what we say about Jesus. And God's colorful kingdom will grow.

Prayer Pointer

Jesus, please help me follow Your lead by loving others well and telling others about Your goodness.

Hot Mess

> "A person speaks the things
> that are in his heart."
>
> Luke 6:45

D id you know that one of the most beautiful places on earth is also home to the tallest mountain in the world? Hawaii's Mauna Loa measures over thirteen thousand feet from its base deep within the Pacific Ocean to its highest peak. How did it get so tall? Well, it's no ordinary mountain. It's a volcano that built itself to grand heights with the many eruptions that have occurred over time.

Even though Mauna Loa looks like a regular mountain on the outside, deep inside its core, magma (liquid, burning rock) pools and builds. When rock plates in the earth's crust shift, the magma gets squeezed to the top, overflowing the mountain's sides. Though it may be exciting, eruptions can cause terrible consequences, such as mudslides, avalanches, flash floods, and earthquakes.

Volcanoes are powerful reminders to us that what lies on the inside is even more important than how something looks on the outside. Someone could be gorgeous on the outside, but if her heart is full of explosive anger, self-centeredness, or other sin, it can ruin everything. That's why God cares so much about what's going on inside our hearts and minds. He wants us to be full of His love so that we overflow with the beautiful words and actions of His Spirit.

Prayer Pointer

Lord, please make me beautiful from the inside
out by the power of Your Holy Spirit.

> ### THe LoRd gives sleep to tHose He loves.
> #### Psalm 127:2

Want to be really active? Then get some sleep! God created our bodies to need sleep so that our cells can prepare us for the next day. For example, while our brains are shutting down our voluntary muscles so they can rest while we sleep, our brains are also firing off thoughts to clear our minds and create new pathways for memory and learning. During deep sleep, the brain releases hormones that help us kids grow taller and stronger. All our cells are refueled for the next day if we get enough good sleep. But without it, we immediately feel the effects: anger, mood swings, sad thoughts, tiredness, and just not being interested in the day's activities. Losing sleep over a long period of time can even hurt your heart, cause growth delays, and lead to obesity. Sleep is important!

The same is true for us spiritually. God has given us bodies that are designed to be really active in sharing the gospel and helping others. But we do that best when we rest from trying to do everything on our own. Instead, we ask and trust God to change us, make us new, and use us to show His glory. He will renew our minds and fuel our bodies to take on the challenges of each new day.

PRayeR PoiNteR

God, thank You that I can rest in the love of Jesus, knowing that His Spirit will fuel me and lead me to do Your will.

Caught by Beauty

It is the evil that a person wants that
tempts him. . . . This desire causes sin.
Then the sin grows and brings death.

James 1:14–15

If you hate spiders, move to Antarctica—it's the only place in the world without them. Everywhere else, you are out of luck! Did you know there are more than forty thousand different species of spiders? Most of us find them creepy, but they are actually very valuable because they help pollinate plants, keep the pesky insect population down, and are a great source of food for birds, lizards, and other creatures. Some kinds, like the wolf spider or the giant huntsman spider (with a leg span of one foot!), chase their prey to capture it. But most spiders use the spinnerets on their abdomens to create silk, which they weave into a sticky web to catch their meals.

Those webs can look beautiful, but watching a spider wrap and eat its prey on that web can be horrifying. How can something so beautiful be so deadly? God says that sin operates the same way for us. It often looks beautiful and inviting at first, but sin is a trap just like a spider's web. It can lead to spiritual death. The good news is that Jesus frees us from its grip through His forgiveness and love. Stay away from sticky sin, and stick with Jesus instead!

Prayer Pointer

Jesus, help me stay away from the trap
of sin, and keep me close to You.

You are young, but do not let anyone treat you
as if you were not important. Be an example
to show the believers how they should live.

1 Timothy 4:12

Have you ever seen a male peacock fanning his tail feathers to show off his rainbow of colors? Now picture all those brilliant colors poured into a cool pattern on a *shrimp*. Sound impossible? Not if you've seen the peacock mantis shrimp. Not only is the peacock mantis shrimp colorful on the outside, but it has two eyes (which move independently of each other) that can see ten times more color than human eyes can. Oh, and another thing—these little guys are fast. They can propel themselves through the water at speeds so fast your eyes can hardly see them, causing deadly damage to the crabs or mollusks they are hunting.

So what would the peacock mantis shrimp tell you, if it could? Probably that you shouldn't worry about your size or shape or age. God has designed you to bring beauty and color and brilliant energy into the world just by being who you are and doing what you do. When you love God and trust the direction He has for your life, you are bound to have tremendous impact as He propels you to bring life and love to everyone around you.

Prayer Pointer

Lord, I trust that You have the power to use someone
small like me to do big things with You.

Beauty in Progress

God began doing a good work in you.
And He will continue it until it is finished
when Jesus Christ comes again.

Philippians 1:6

D o you ever look in the mirror and wish you were older? Or kinder? Or a better friend? Sometimes it seems like we are never going to grow up or figure out how to be the people God wants us to be.

That's why God made caterpillars. Okay, it's maybe not the *only* reason, but caterpillars' lives can give us a little insight into how God changes us too. Caterpillars creep around on their stubby legs, eating whatever they can until the time comes for them to start forming a cocoon. Then they lie in their cocoons while an amazing transformation takes place. When they wake up from their long sleep, they scratch through their cocoons and come out into the world as beautiful butterflies (or moths, depending on the type of caterpillar).

Right now you might not feel as though you are important or special, but you are! God is working in your heart at this very moment, slowly transforming you to become more like Jesus. Just like the caterpillar rests while nature does its work, we can rest from trying to become something that we aren't . . . yet. Instead, we trust that God is at work and that He is making us into the beautiful people He has created us to be!

Prayer Pointer

Jesus, help me be patient as You work in me to
make me beautiful for You.

My darling, you are beautiful!
Oh, you are beautiful!

Song of Songs 1:15

So how is beauty defined? It depends on where you live. Here in the United States, the media prizes slender girls with flawless skin, big eyes, and long hair. But if you lived in the Pa Dong tribe near Thailand, you'd want a long neck—a look you can only achieve by adding metal rings around your neck year after year, starting at age six. If you lived in New Zealand with the Maori women, you would value tattooed blue lips. People in Mauritania and Nigeria would feel sorry for skinny American girls, since they believe the bigger the woman is, the more beautiful she is!

The truth is, our ideas about what is in style or what looks good comes from what other people around us say—and those ideas change all the time. Trying to meet everybody else's expectations is not only exhausting, it's silly! We were made to show our Creator's creativity and love through our different looks, personalities, and style as we live a life all about loving others—not by trying to look and act like everybody around us. The Bible says to stop comparing yourself with other people, stop trying to be like them or better than them. Instead, God says to be bold, brave, and *be-you-tiful*!

Prayer Pointer

Father, You have told me in so many ways that I am beautiful to You. Please help me to listen only to You!